W9-BGS-847

Twirling Naked in the Streets—and No One Noticed

GROWING UP WITH UNDIAGNOSED AUTISM

JEANNIE DAVIDE-RIVERA

David and Goliath Publishing

www.davidandgoliathpublishing.com

Copyright © 2012 Jeannie Davide-Rivera

All rights reserved.

ISBN-10: 0615801439
ISBN-13: 978-0615801438

DEDICATION

To my husband Mark, and my three boys Adam, Matthew, and Thomas

Table of Contents

Acknowledgements

I want to thank first and foremost my husband Mark without whom I would not have been able to complete this book. Thank you for your dedication and commitment to our lives, our family, and your constant encouragement.

A special thanks to Dr. Sasha Federer, who was the first psychologist to truly see me, who listened to me, and offered constant encouragement and guidance throughout my writing process.

.

Introduction

In 1974, 1 in 5,000 children were diagnosed with autism. When I began writing this book in 2012, that number was estimated at 1 in 88. In early 2013, the Center for Disease Control (CDC) released yet another statistic; 1 in 55 children are now diagnosed and identified as being on the autism spectrum. What has changed? Are there more autistic children being born now than ever before? Is there an epidemic?

I believe the reason for the rising autism rates is two-fold. First, physicians are trained more thoroughly and recognize the symptoms that were once lost on many of us as children, and secondly, the diagnostic criterion has changed drastically over the years. The new diagnostic criterion allows doctors to recognize more children, and adults, on the spectrum. The more that is learned about autism, the more these parameters have and will continue to be changed.

The idea that only 1 in 5,000 children had autism in 1974 I believe is a gross underestimation. The fact is that autistic children were indeed in your midst then; however, doctors, teachers, and parents alike did not recognize the autism. When I was growing up autism was narrowly defined. In order to be diagnosed with autism you had to be unable to speak, and have a lower than average I.Q. Today, we know this to be false.

In fact, those on the higher functioning side of the spectrum, those with Asperger's Syndrome not only can speak but often could speak very early, and profoundly. To complicate matters further these same children were labeled gifted, spoiled, too smart for their own good, and the list goes on. Many children with Asperger's Syndrome not only have average I.Q.'s but many have I.Q's that are well above average. What happened to all these children who were intelligent, verbal, but still struggled because they indeed were autistic? They became adults.

In 1994, Asperger's Syndrome (AS) was added to the *Diagnostic and Statistical Manual of Mental Disorders IV* (DSM-IV), and recognized as part of the autism spectrum. Although, autism is a neurological disorder, it continues to be classified in DSM's. According to the DSM-IV, in order to be diagnosed with AS a child or adult must display "qualitative impairment in social interaction, as manifested by at least two of the following:

1. Marked impairment in the use of multiple nonverbal behaviors such as eye-to-eye gaze, facial expression, body postures, and gestures to regulate social interaction.
2. Failure to develop peer relationships appropriate to developmental level
3. A lack of spontaneous seeking to share enjoyment, interests, or achievements with other people, or
4. A lack of social or emotional reciprocity

In addition the individual must display one of the following restrictive repetitive and stereotyped patterns of behavior, interests and activities, as manifested by at least one of the following:

1. An encompassing preoccupation with one or more stereotyped and restricted patterns of interest that is abnormal in either intensity or focus.
2. An apparently inflexible adherence to specific, nonfunctional routines or rituals.

3. Stereotyped and repetitive motor mannerisms, such as hand or finger tapping, twisting, or whole-body movements.
4. Persistent preoccupation with parts of objects."

A diagnosis of Asperger's Syndrome also requires that these disturbances impair social, occupation or other areas of functioning. There can be no language delay, and no delay in cognitive development. In other words, AS was now being recognized as a part of the autism spectrum. Prior to 1994, these children and adults went undiagnosed—they were missed.

I was one of those missed children, and became one of the missed adults; this is my story.

Chapter One: They Missed It; They Missed Me

I am a survivor; an autism survivor.

I have been torn down, pulled to pieces, and have had my heart ripped from my chest slammed on the floor and stomped into the ground. But—I am still here to tell about it.

I grew up in a world before autism advocacy; born twenty years before Asperger's Syndrome was acknowledged in the U.S. I now hear talk about autism being an epidemic. There are more autistic children being identified than ever before. I've heard people say that they didn't see many autistic children when they were growing up, but I am here to tell you that we indeed were in your midst.

My parents did not notice, my teachers were blind to it, and my doctor's misdiagnosed it. When they noticed me on tip-toes, they made me a ballerina. When I twirled round and round, I was only dancing. When I had imaginary friends, they said that was just what little girls did.

When the light bothered me, I was allergic to sunlight. When smells overwhelmed me, I had a sensitive stomach. When I only ate a few select items, I was picky. When I could not stray from my rigid routine, I was hard-headed.

When I thought I was smarter than my teachers, I was obnoxious. When I couldn't stand certain fabrics touching my body, I was being a princess. When I cried and screamed, I was spoiled. When I rocked back and forth, I was concentrating. When I sat alone, I was in my own world.

When I couldn't keep up, I was not living up to my potential. When I didn't think the way others did, I was just too smart for my own good. When I didn't connect with my peers, I just didn't care about them. When I misinterpreted situations, I was inconsiderate. When I asserted myself, I was inappropriate.

When the children's screaming hurt my head, I was a bad mother. When I could not keep them on a schedule, or keep the house in tip-top shape, I was lazy. When I could not stick to a budget, I was irresponsible. When I couldn't understand, I was stupid.

When I stayed in my pajamas for days, I was depressed. When I was overwhelmed by the world, I was agoraphobic. When I was tired and frightened, I had an anxiety disorder. When I realized something was wrong with me, I was making excuses.

The one thing my entire life's experiences screamed, the one thing that was consistent, was that everything was *my fault*.

No one recognized my autism; no one saw that I had Asperger's Syndrome. How could they? Asperger's Syndrome, Aspies—I – did not exist; not yet.

Imaginary Friends and Obsessions

Autistic children do not participate in imaginary play. What about imaginary friends?

My friends were old men with bats.

Do imaginary friends fall into the category of imaginary play, or can they come about because of special interests and obsessions?

Some say that our imaginary friends present themselves in reaction to our loneliness and isolation. But when I had my imaginary friends, I was too young and oblivious to know I was isolated and lonely. I was not yet three-years-old.

Some of my earliest memories were of my imaginary friends, but those friends were "real" people who were a part of my very first all-consuming special interest—baseball.

I was born in the spring of 1974 in Brooklyn, New York, to an avid Yankee fan. My father and I watched ballgames every time they were televised. He would lay in bed watching our small black and white television while I lay sprawled across the foot of the bed engrossed in the game. I had to watch my friends play.

By the time I was three years old, I memorized the entire Yankee line-up, including stats. Dad was proud of my fact memorizing capabilities.

When my father could not throw the ball back and forth with me in the driveway, my baseball men were there to help with my training. I was obsessed with baseball, I was obsessed with the Yankees, and I was obsessed with my baseball men. They were my friends.

I did not leave the house, our family did not go on vacation, or to a restaurant, or anywhere without Reggie Jackson, Catfish Hunter, and Thurman Munster in tow. They couldn't, or it would have caused a complete meltdown, resulting in my screaming and crying. They even had assigned seats in the back of our car. When my brother John was born, the baseball men had to sit on each other's laps in order to fit—and there had to be room for my ten puppies.

Yes—I also traveled with ten imaginary puppies, and like my baseball men there was no leaving them home.

One day our car got a flat, and my father had to pull-over to change the tire on the side of the Belt Parkway. When he opened the door a few of my puppies scurried out with him to keep him company. When my father was finished, he hopped back into the car and we were on our way.

As the story is retold, I only have a vague memory of this event; as soon as we started down the parkway they (my parents) heard a blood-curling scream coming out of the back seat. My father thought that maybe I had got my finger caught in the door or something. That wasn't it. He left three of my puppies on the side of the road!

Unable to calm me down, he had to get off at the next exit and head back. My Dad walked through the grass to find my imaginary puppies—there were only two there. He lost one. I was inconsolable until the baseball men, who were also off in the grass on the side of the Belt Parkway leading their own search and rescue team, returned with puppy number ten.

Everyone returned to their assigned seats, I lined up my ten puppies across the floor at my feet, and Dad was allowed to continue our journey to my grandmother's house in Queens.

"You had your father roaming through the grass looking for imaginary puppies just to shut you up," my mother said.

There isn't much else I can recall about those puppies. Maybe they grew up and it was time for them to be on their own, or maybe they just fell by the way side as baseball became the most important thing in my universe.

"I don't have any narrowly focused special interests, no all-consuming obsessions—not during childhood."

I protested my diagnosis, but only for a moment. I was a baseball obsessed pre-schooler.

I knew all the players; I knew their numbers.

I knew the line-up; I knew all the stats.

I knew the TV airtimes; I didn't miss a game.

I knew the route to Cooperstown, New York, where the Baseball Hall of Fame is located, although, we never made the trip. I had a map.

Baseball was my obsession. I was four years old.

During "practice," the times that my father and I played ball in the driveway, I was coached by one of my three baseball men. Dad and I threw the ball back and forth. When I threw to him I was pitching and Catfish was right there telling me how to stand, where to look, and how to lift up my leg like he does on the mound at the stadium.

When Dad threw the ball to me, I was a catcher. I did not stand up straight like other children did to catch the ball. I crouched down as per instructed by Thurmon. I positioned my glove between my legs, adjusted my imaginary face plate, and prepared to catch the ball. I was extraordinarily talented according to my "coaches," my "friends." I was not a modest child.

Since I needed pitching and catching coaches, it makes sense that I chose a batter from the team to coach me when it was my turn to hit. Reggie taught me how to stand with my feet squarely facing home plate, where to position my hands on the bat, and continually reminded me to keep my eye on the ball.

I wonder what my father's role in all our baseball playing was. Did he know he was just the guy who needed to throw that ball to me, catch when I pitched it back, and run after the balls I hit with the bat like Lou Piniella did in the outfield—or like Graig Nettles, number 9, on third base? My coaches taught me everything I needed to know about baseball—at least in my mind they did.

In return for all their help, my three baseball men accompanied us on family outings, ate dinner with us, and I often was report to be making them hot dogs for lunch. This is also when my extensive baseball card collection began, Yankees only of course.

1979 was a sad year for baseball. Thurmon Munson died in plane crash, and Catfish Hunter retired. Two of my three baseball men were gone. My imaginary friends did not outlive their physical lives, or their Yankee baseball careers for that matter. But—1979 was the year the Yankees picked up Dave Righetti.

Dave Righetti; number 19.

Righetti started pitching for the New York Yankees in 1979, and although he did not become one of my imaginary friends, he rapidly became my favorite player. In 1981, Dave Righetti was assigned number 19, the day of my birth, thus started my lifelong obsession with the number 19.

I was wrong. I did have special interests and all-consuming obsessions   even   when   I   was   very   young.

Chapter Two: The Little Encyclopedia; Consuming Information and Hyperlexia

Before 1994, Asperger's Syndrome did not exist as a diagnosis in the United States. Autism would not have even been considered if a child was verbal, least of all *very* verbal, or if a child was not intellectually challenged.

I was verbal, *too* verbal. I was smart, *too* smart for my own good.

Baseball stats were not the only bits of data that I consumed and stored. I consumed books. I memorized them, and don't you dare read the storybook to me and think you will skip over anything. If I had already heard the book, you were in trouble.

My father used to read to me, but many times tried to skip over things thinking I wouldn't know any better. After all, I couldn't read—or, could I?

I would promptly point out what he missed along with the page the text appeared on. Long before I entered kindergarten I didn't need him to read to me any longer. I taught myself to read.

I honestly could not figure out why we were "learning" to read in school. I already knew how to read; therefore, all the kids around me knew also. We were just wasting time.

"We thought we had a little genius on our hands," my mother said, "but you were just a little bitch." That is the way my mother described me. She had no idea I was hyperlexic.

What is hyperlexia?

Hyperlexia is an ability to read way above what is expected for the child's age, and is accompanied by a below average ability to comprehend spoken language. The hyperlexic child usually learns to speak through rote memory and heavy repetition. This child appears (and is) very intelligent, but often fails to comprehend the context of their words, or fails to comprehend their meanings and social implications.

I was not a quiet withdrawn child; in fact, I never shut up— ever. I rattled off my newly learned facts to anyone who would listen, and to those who wouldn't. The interesting part though is I would only talk to adults. Children had nothing to contribute to the conversation; they thought I was odd. Sometimes they ran from me, or they ran off to play.

Adults, on the other hand, thought I was brilliant. They laughed at my little speeches, and thought it was cute when I recited lines from TV shows and music lyrics to answer their questions. Well—most of the time.

There were times when my tendency to quote others to convey my feelings landed me in a heap of trouble. As "grown-up" as I sounded at almost four years old, I still had my bottle. It was something I was absolutely unwilling to give up. The doctors were not concerned, and actually encouraged my parents to allow me to have it as long as I wanted since I ate next to nothing.

"Milk is food," Grandma said. So why would I need to eat anything else. My father, however, didn't share this view.

When he insisted that I eat the dinner my mother prepared, I, as always, refused. This time he persisted.

"You are going to eat it," he said.

"Why?"

"Because I said so, now eat it!" I had somehow made him angry, but not as angry as he made me. Maybe he shouldn't have played so much Billy Joel music around me; he should have seen this coming.

"You cannot tell me what to do. It's my life!" I said. "Go ahead with your own life, leave me alone!"

I ran up the stairs, clutching my bottle in my hand.

My grandparents lived on the second floor of our two-family home. Grandma says milk is food. I don't need to eat my mother's food, I have my own.

This time Grandma was on *their* side. She wanted me to eat. I sniffed the pasta, I sniffed the meatballs, and I sniffed the cheese, and then I wretched.

"No! I don't want your stinky cheese; I don't need your stinky cheese; I have my bottle. Milk is food!"

That was the last time I saw that bottle, or any other ones. So for the next year I lived on peanut butter.

There were times when my speech and comprehension appeared advanced. It may have appeared to my parents that I was being obstinate and difficult—that I only wanted my way. But the truth is I had no idea the real implications and meanings behind the words I recited from the song, *My Life*. It just appeared that I applied it correctly at the time.

Since I was already able to read, I often used "scripts" to speak to people. I recited passages from books that seemed appropriate at the time. I sang song lyrics, or in this case, screamed song lyrics at others. I also repeated what I heard adults saying applying it to my situations haphazardly. Because I was smart, everyone assumed that the words were my own, my thoughts, and that I knew exactly what I was saying. I am sure I did not.

My grandparents owned a house in upstate New York, in Sullivan County, their weekend home. It was a three hour drive from our house in Brooklyn.

Every Friday night right after my father came home from work we packed our things in the car and headed upstate. As soon as we crossed the Hudson and headed up into the mountains it started; they knew it was coming.

My eyes grew wide as I watched the mountains come into view. Soon the road would be going up and down. I waited for it.

As the car started driving on an incline I started.

"Up the hill."

The other side brought a decline.

"Down the hill."

A steeper hill warranted a louder voice, "UP THE HILL." And a deep drop—a softer voice, "down the hill." On our way, "up the hill," my head leaned back so I can look up into the sky. On our way, "down the hill," my head sagged forward to look down to the floor.

"The whole way there—you drove us crazy," my mother said.

The only thing that ever changed during the trip was the volume of my voice. This continued for the rest of the trip into the mountains—for two more hours, each and every time we drove there.

These car rides into the country were worse for my parents if my Uncle Patrick came along. He made me sick. If he was sitting in the backseat with me, I would vomit before I made it to my hills. Soon, I rode upstate with my grandparents.

It took me a long time to figure out why my uncle Pat made me sick. He smelled like motor oil. No matter how many times he washed his hands the grease from working on his cars did not completely come off, and I could smell it. Even now, I cannot stomach the smell of motor oil. I will avoid mechanic's shops at all costs.

My "up the hill, down the hill," routine lasted for many years. When I grew older I learned to whisper it to myself, and avoid the smack that would inevitably come from the front seat.

Mom decided there was nothing wrong with me. I just wanted my own way; to be stubborn; to be "a little bitch".

There is not a time I can remember that I didn't have the need to feel and touch everything before putting it on, or smell something before eating it. It was not a choice; it was a compulsion. I had to, but the question is why?

On my sixth birthday I was happily tearing through the wrapping paper to get to my gifts. I already knew what was inside most of the boxes, because I hated surprises.

My parents had learned to take me to the store to pick out my own gifts because if I didn't like the looks of something, I would not touch it. I was picky—about everything, but it was more than that.

Dad would take me shopping and let me choose a gift, bring it home and wrap it. I never complained about having to wait to open my presents, a week, or even a month was fine so long as I knew what was in the box before I opened it.

When it came time to open a gift from my godmother, I tore through the paper as usual, but I was already worried. I had no idea what that box contained. I needed to know—ahead of time. I carefully lifted the top off the box and peered inside.

"I'm not wearing those, take them back to the store."

My mother face reddened. "You are going to wear them," she said through gritted teeth. "Say thank you."

"Thank you. Can you take them back?"

My mother was furious. She insisted that my godmother not return the shirts and that I was indeed going to wear them. I never did.

Several days earlier my mother and father had a huge fight.

"You always spoil her, and let her get her own way!"

Dad took me to Toys R Us to pick out a birthday present. We walked up and down the isles looking for the Barbie head. Do you remember the Barbie head? Barbie's head was bigger than my own, with long blond hair that cascaded over the shoulders. It came complete with brushes and make-up.

I wanted her—not to play with her of course, just to sit her on my dresser in my room. Maybe she would be another imaginary friend. I could arrange her things, brushes, make-up, and even give her a hat if it was cold outside.

"What is wrong with you? This is why she's spoiled!" she yelled. "Twenty-five dollars for something she is not even going to play with."

I will never forget my sixth birthday, and the venom that my mother spewed toward my father for allowing me to pick out my own gift—for spoiling me, for giving in, for letting me have my own way. Why did she hate me so much?

What was wrong with the shirts? Why did I dig my heels in and refuse to wear them knowing it would bring my mother's wrath? Did I just want to aggravate her?

The shirts felt funny. I could tell just by looking at them. And they were multi-colored stripes—dizzying.

"You can't tell how something will feel by looking at it. You never even touched the shirts before being nasty and telling your godmother to return them. You just didn't like them," my mother said. More than thirty years later she is still telling the story of what a nasty ungrateful child I was.

Even now when I stroll through a store shopping for clothing, which I hate doing, I go directly to the items that "look" like they will feel good. I shop by touching the fabric, running my hands back and forth over it, and then rubbing it on my cheeks. Sometimes, I look like a crazy woman.

If I get ahold of a soft blanket or furry throw pillow, I catch myself toting it around like a security blanket, especially if I am stressed, or in a large overwhelming store. I suppose I may have learned to shop this way—from my grandmother.

Grandma made my dresses. She made my hats, scarfs, gloves, and sweaters for winter. I could not wear any store bought ones, they were scratchy and I tore them off. The wool made me itch. My skin became red and blotchy, and I would scratch until I bled. Grandma's clothes were soft.

Holding my hand, Grandma and I walked down 18th avenue where I grew up in Brooklyn. We crossed the four lanes of traffic at 65th street when the light said it was safe to do so (we followed the rules); walked past Da Vinci's pizzeria on or way to the fabric store where Grandma bought her yarn. Sometimes we stopped along the way so I could go on the quarter rides sitting in front of the store windows. I liked to walk to the fabric store—the avenue smelled good.

I loved the smells coming from the bakery. Fresh baked Italian bread, and cookies. We always stopped for cookies—amaretto cookies. The smell of baked cheeses and tomato sauce floated out of the pizzerias. I liked how the cheese sizzled and the sauce bubbled on the round pies that came out of the oven, and then slid onto the pizza trays. I loved everything about the trips to the fabric store.

Grandma roamed up and down the narrow aisles searching for the right yarn.

"Do you like this one?" she asked handing me a fluffy ball.

I rubbed it on my cheek, nodded, and continued following behind her. Grandma went up and down the aisles until we collected enough of those tiny balls of yarn for my sweater.

"Making a baby blanket?" the woman behind the register asked.

"No, a sweater for my granddaughter" Grandma said pointed to me.

The woman's eyebrows arched upward like two arrows pointing up to the sky. I looked up wondering what they were pointing at. Why was she making that odd face?

"She has expensive taste," grandma said, a smile spreading crossed her face, "just like mine." Then she paid the lady with the arrow eyebrows, and we were on our way.

My new sweater would be soft. There would be no itching, no scratching, no tearing it off my body, and no tags!

"You tore out all your tags so I never knew what size anything was."

~ Mom

I did; I tore them all out—out of every piece of clothing I owned. If the item was tolerable, the tag had to go because it was not. I knew the trouble the hole left by the tag would get me into. It didn't matter. There was no discussing it. I had no choice. The tag had to go!

To me the hole left behind was a good thing. It was a mark indicating that I would wear the clothes—my mark of approval. I guess my mother didn't see it that way.

Attempts to force me to wear clothing I couldn't tolerate resulted in a naked kid. I didn't mind being naked either, in fact, I preferred it.

Ripping my clothes off started as soon as I was able to wriggle out of my cloth diaper and take off running through the house. My mother thought she was fortunate; she began having babies when new disposable diapers were all the rage. It's too bad that I could not wear them.

Even as an infant I was hyper-sensitive; I had tactile sensitivities. My skin blistered under the disposable diapers so the doctor determined that I must be allergic to them. Allergies were used to explain away many of my sensitivities throughout my childhood.

If my mother forced me to wear the clothes that I didn't *want* to, I would wind up just taking them off and leaving them somewhere in the street. In the cold New York City winters tossing your hat and scarf into the street to be rid of them makes for an icicle child. I think that my mother would have just let me freeze until I learned to not throw away my mittens, but grandma didn't want me to get sick. She continued to make my winter bundles.

I was not the most organized child; actually, I was a mess.

"You would lose your head if it wasn't attached." ~Mom

She was right. I lost everything including my grandmother's handmade hats, scarfs, gloves, and sweaters. I lost them all the time. It is a good thing grandma could knit very quickly, and always had extras on hand. She spent hours and hours (usually alone) knitting away. I didn't realize until much later how incredible expensive it was to make my angora scarves.

Maybe she started putting tags into my things to shut my mother up, so my clothes would have a tag in them to write a size down on. Or, maybe it was so I could recover some of my hats—so the lost and found at school would know they were mine.

Grandma began sewing her own custom made tags on the inside of my things. I remember her designing and ordering the tags from a company who specialized in custom clothing items. The tags were made of a soft sateen white material. The baby blue embroidery (I liked everything to be blue.) said:

Especially Made By Grandma for _____.

Now there was a place to put my name on my clothes, and yes—a size too.

Grandma carefully sewed each tag in by hand, weaving in and out of the fabric with silken thread. She made sure to sew them completely flat so the tag did not stick up to irritate my skin.

Chapter Three: The Princess, Her Socks, and Her Late Pass

"You tried on ten pairs of socks every morning before deciding which pair you would wear" ~ *Mom*

I hate socks. I hate the way they feel on my feet, the way they bunch up in my shoes, and how the seams rub against my toes when I walk. Socks make me hot. When I'm overheated the first thing I need to do is rip them off—now.

To make matters worse my mother liked to buy thin nylon socks trimmed with lace. Not many materials irritate me more than scratchy lace. The thin nylon socks made my feet sweaty. My feet slid around inside my hard patent leather school shoes. They were not good shoes for a clumsy kindergartner.

When I finally found a pair of socks that I could wear, they usually did not match. Mom insisted that I just didn't like any of the socks, but if that was the case then why did I need to try each pair on? Why did I need to see how they felt on my feet? Wouldn't I have just flat out refused to put them on because I didn't like them?

By the time I was dressed, and my three year old brother was in the carriage, we were rushing to make it to school on time.

"You could not make Jeannie move fast." ~ Mom

Every morning the three of us set out to walk the five blocks to school. We headed up the avenue in the opposite direction of Grandma's fabric store. We walked past the pork store, my favorite candy store, which was still closed and covered with a steel shutter, past the bagel store, the Becker's carpet shop, and across 61st street with the crossing guard waving us onward.

"Jeannie you're going to be late," Mom said. I had stopped short in front of the side entrance to the school. My mother turned to the right heading toward the schoolyard where the kindergarteners entered, and I turned left.

"You can still go in through the schoolyard," Mom said.

I said nothing, stayed the path, and marched around the corner heading for the front entrance; Mom followed.

I stepped inside the door just when the bell rang.

"Good Morning, Jeannie," a woman's voice said from the small desk that sat just to the left side of the entrance. I kept walking.

My mother was still wrestling my brother out of his carriage when I started climbing the towering steps. When I reached the first landing I stopped and stooped down.

"Hurry up Jeannie, you're late," the woman's voice came from below.

"I have to fix my shoes."

When I was satisfied with my adjustments, I continued my ascent to the first floor, and marched to the main office.

I walked straight past the ladies behind the desk, around the counter, past the school secretary, and into the principal's office.

Mr. Hiler was a huge man; he towered over me, his head reaching almost to the ceiling when he stood up.

"Hello Jeannie," he said walking out from behind his desk. He handed me a small piece of paper all ready and waiting for me. I hopped up into the seat in front of his desk.

"She still won't come in through the school yard," mother said. She was slightly out of breath from toting my brother up the stairs on her hip.

Mr. Hiler smiled; mother did not.

"Why won't you come in through the schoolyard?" he asked.

"She just wants to be late, "mother said.

"I have to see Mr. Hiler for my late pass."

"You wouldn't need a late pass if you went in the other way," mom argued.

"I need to see Mr. Hiler for my late pass!" I said in a slightly louder voice than before to make my point clearer. Mom's face turned red. *Why does her face turn that color?*

"It's alright, Jeannie can come to see me whenever she likes," Mr. Hiler said. "Now off to class, Mrs. Divine is waiting for you."

I smiled, and walked out of his office scowling at my mother as I went by. *Why didn't she understand? She knows I have to get my late pass.*

To my mother, I was just being difficult; I wanted to do things my own way. I had a mind of my own and no one was going to change it—ever.

This scene played itself over and over again. The leaves dried up, snow fell, flowers bloomed, and days changed. My patent leather shoes changed into snow boots, and my boots to sandals, but the routine never changed. I marched to the front entrance, up the stairs to the landing, fixed my shoes, walked into the office, ignored the ladies, and drifted into Mr. Hiler's office to retrieve my late pass. Then, and only then, did I go to see Mrs. Divine, my kindergarten teacher.

Mr. Hiler's words, *Jeannie can come to see me whenever she likes*, proved troublesome for years to come.

Looking back I now know my morning sock routine was due to tactile sensitivities. I needed to find a pair I could tolerate. I know this because I am the same today about my socks. What about the rest of my routine? Was my pause to fix my shoes on the landing born from the socks and shoes being irritating? Why did I only fix them on that landing—every single day without deviation for the entire school year?

I could not stray from that routine. I suspect that it was the routine I adopted on the first day of school, and that was how every day of school thereafter *had* to go. Yes—I was late on my first day of kindergarten because of the rocks in my socks that no one could find.

As an adult I find myself adhering to very similar patterns of behavior. If I unpack boxes from a move and put something away it is very difficult for me to move it. That becomes its place, and it always lives there even if it is not where I want it. It is important for me to unpack and arrange my things thoughtfully the first time because wherever I place the toaster is where it is going to stay. That initial placing, the initial routine becomes set in stone.

It's a good thing that kindergarten was only a half-day or the other kids may not have survived. I am told that I did not share well, but the truth of it is that I was not trying to keep all the toys for myself. I just didn't want anyone to mess them up. I tried to help the other children play, to do it the right way, but they couldn't learn.

The block corner was my favorite place to be. The only problem was that it was popular with the other kids as well. I spent most of my time stacking the blocks—carefully piling them high into the sky. I remember trying to make skyscrapers like the ones I watched whiz by from the backseat of my father's 1979 baby blue Cadillac. As soon as Dad got on the up-ramp to the Brooklyn Queens Expressway (BQE) I watched for them, then I hopped to my knees and watched out the rear window until they were completely out of sight.

Skyscrapers are not meant to fall; not meant to be knocked over by giggling boys who wanted to kick their pieces and throw them around like footballs. Blocks were meant for building—so I built, and built, and built.

If only the school had enough blocks for my skyscrapers and for the other children everything would have been perfect—maybe. I couldn't let them touch the blocks, they weren't doing it right. I tried to teach them the right way to stack blocks. I wanted their help building, I did, but they just couldn't get it right.

When one of the boys in my class decided it was his turn, and tried to destroy my building in order to get his meaty hands on my precious blocks, I clawed him.

I dug my fingernails into his spongy flesh, and dragged it down the top of his hands. He screamed, he bled, and he let go of my block.

By the time the teacher was beside us, I was already

engrossed with rebuilding the roof that he so carelessly ripped off.

I don't know why scratching became my weapon of choice. Maybe it was because I was so tiny and could never overpower one of the other kids. I was number three, which means there were only two children smaller than me; Toni and Laura. Shayne was number 4, he stood right behind me. Those three never got clawed, not that I can remember anyway, it was always the bigger ones.

Kindergarten should only have one activity per day; that way we wouldn't have to change activities. Even now I cannot switch activities easily. If I am interrupted it is impossible to resume what I was doing without delay. My brain needs time to make the switch.

When I am writing, as I am today, and the phone rings, or the kids interrupt, it takes a few minutes to even process what they are asking me. Most of the time I am angered by the interruption, and I am an adult.

Part of the problem is that I get so engrossed in what I am doing that I forget about the world around me. The interruption becomes an unexpected intrusion. To compound the problem, getting back to my activity can take some time. Depending on the nature of the interruption resuming can take anywhere from a few minutes to several hours; it is never instantaneous. This makes switching from one activity to the next difficult and time consuming.

When we were required to switch play centers, and I was moved from the blocks to the play kitchen, I could not do it. I could not run and play house without finishing what I was working on. I didn't refuse, I wasn't trying to be ornery, I just didn't move.

If a switch was successful, I would spend all of my "play" time re-arranging the house area. They did not have the kitchen set up right; the eggs belong in the refrigerator not in the cabinet! I had no interest in pretending to play house, only in arranging things to be in their proper order. While the other girls and boys played mommies, and daddies, I fixed the cupboard. The girls toted baby dolls around, and I fretted about who moved the plastic bananas. *Where exactly had they moved them to anyway? Why would they put them in there?*

I never did consider that there could be more than one right way to set up the kitchen; there wasn't.

I realize now that my "play" was always modeled after real life—only better, more orderly, and more predictable—unless of course, others were involved.

I did not build rocket ships that launched off to Mars; no one went to Mars! I did not play with dolls pretending they were babies; they were plastic. There was this one doll though, one doll that I had to have—the Joey doll.

My grandfather watched Archie Bunker in the TV show "All in the Family" every night, which meant so did I. Joey was Archie Bunker's grandson. Baby Joey was a controversial doll; he was the first doll to be just like a real baby. Joey was anatomically correct! *Just like a real baby? OK—I can do that.*

First lesson in anatomy, and the excretory system: put water in Joey's mouth and it comes right out—immediately.

Standing in front of our house, I proudly displayed my stripped Joey doll. "Boys have penises—see! "

I may have traumatized the little old Italian woman in the black dress next door. There were a lot of unrecognizable words coming out of her mouth. Then she made the sign of the cross three times, kissed her crucifix, and rushed off into the house. *What? I thought she knew.*

My fascination with playing at real life did not stop at dolls.

When I played with other children, I always insisted on acting out activities that I did normally.

Growing up we never moved. I didn't leave that house, except episodically, for twenty-five years. For me that made invaluable built-in friends because other families on the block grew up there too. Some are still there today.

When I was very young, I played with three friends on the block: Theresa, Daniella, and Cindy. Theresa and Daniella lived one house away from me. Theresa was two years older than I was, and her family moved there in 1974, the year I was born. I quite literally have known her my entire life. Daniella was two years younger; I think Cynthia was three.

Together we all put on dance recitals in the backyard. Theresa's father grew grapes in their yard to make homemade wine. The grape vines wound around a metal frame that we thought would be perfect for holding a stage curtain.

The three of us carefully set-up the stage by hanging bed sheets and blankets over the grapevines. We practiced, had dress rehearsals, and then invited our parents to the shows. We collected music, dressed in tutus, and twirled around like the ballerinas we were. I wonder if they ever tired of our shows. We seem to always be putting on a show, and many times to an empty audience.

I had an obsession with walking on my tiptoes—I always did. I'm told that I walked on my toes everywhere I went especially when I was very young. My grandparents had a Pianola in their living room. A Pianola played music all on its own; it was like magic. Grandpa would unroll paper scrolls dotted with small holes, and put them into a secret compartment on the front of the piano.

He slid the cherry wood door to the compartment shut, and flipped the golden switch. The piano jumped to life. The keys bounced up and down on their own, the foot petal tapped by itself like there was a ghost sitting playing. The ghost played beautiful music. I could twirl round and round for hours to the velvety music that filled the room—and I did.

"She has ballerina feet," Grandma said. "Look at her twirl, she's a natural." And so, off to ballet class I went.

I loved ballet class. For the clumsy mess that I was outside the dance studio it is a real wonder how I didn't severely hurt myself dancing. When I was dancing, and twirling, and listening to the music, I could drown the world out. Everything disappeared; there was only the flow of the music. I loved the sound of the piano.

An intense focus allowed me to dance without mistake, because I could not tolerate mistakes. Everything had to be perfect; that is, perfect the way I saw perfect. The only problem was I wanted to dance alone.

I got my wish; my drive for perfection got me noticed. With me it was all or nothing, I saw no point in doing something halfway. I focused on learning my positions, where to place my feet: first position, second position, third, fourth, and fifth. I learned fast, quickly becoming the one who showed others how to do it. This time I could show them the right way, and they listened.

Miss Helen, my dance teacher, was a small older woman with short blond hair. She encouraged me to go around and correct the position of girls' feet. I liked that job. She pulled me to the front of the class to demonstrate, then to lead the class in our routines. It didn't take long for me to memorize them.

Soon I was given solos of my own to perform; I preferred them to dancing with the class. Many times I was granted solos within the class dances, or set out front to do my own routine with them in the background. I was the new little star.

Mom thought I just loved the attention. I loved being helpful, being accurate, being correct, and being able to show others how to do the same. I am starting to see a pattern here—the beginnings of a perfectionist.

I really did want everyone to do things right, not my way, but the right way. Unfortunately, I had no ability to distinguish between the two. There was one right way, I knew what it was, and there was no telling me anything different. I was not very flexible.

I developed an instant love for ballet, and for the classic music that sent me twirling into my own world. I loved the feel of the leotard on my skin. The leotard was smooth, the tights silky, and the ballet slippers hugged my feet. I tried to wear this outfit as often as possible; to play with outside, to dinner, to go shopping, and to school— but my parents drew the line at that one.

Chapter Four: Banished to the Hallways; School Made No Sense

When did I start despising school? I started out loving school. I loved to learn. I loved facts—not to mention that I loved to be right, and to be able to raise my hand and give the correct answer.

By the time I was in second grade school had crushed my love for learning. It was a nightmare full of loud sounds, bright colors, and noisy children. The adoration I received for being "so smart" faded with each grade. I could not understand what was happening. Instead of praise, I was constantly getting reprimanded. Nothing made sense.

Even Mr. Hiler no longer meant what he said. *He said* I could come and see him whenever I wanted, but he lied.

When I got out of my seat, walked out of my classroom, and went down the stairs to the main office to see him, I was in trouble.

"Young lady, you cannot just walk out of Ms. Montouri's class and come down here."

Tears welled up in my eyes as I tried to make sense of it. Ms. Montouri stood in the doorway with her black pointy witch's shoes, furious, and red as a tomato. My mother was on her way up to school.

"Fine!" I finally found my voice, and crossed my arms before stomping off.

"Where are you going?" Ms. Montouri said.

"To the bathroom."

I turned on my heels and marched out of the office, down the hall, and to the girl's bathroom next to the stairs. I sniffed and snorted so that my nose would not run down into my mouth and held back the tears. I was not letting him see me cry, he was a liar.

I stayed curled atop of the bowl in the bathroom and sobbed. *What did I do wrong?*

"You can't just get up and do what you want. You have to listen to your teacher!" mother said.

"But why doesn't she have to listen to me?"

"Because *she's* the teacher"

"I should be teacher then."

I did try to listen to Ms. Montouri after that, even though I didn't understand why I had to. I tried to answer questions in class when I could hear them. Sometimes I even remembered to raise my hand. It's not my fault she didn't see it.

There were a lot of things she did not see. She didn't see Joshua poking me with a pencil, she didn't see him taking my papers, or telling the class if they sat next to me they would get the chicken pox. She didn't see everyone laugh.

I clawed him, I made him bleed, daily—that she saw.

My desk was effectively relocated to the hallway where I could sit by myself and *think about things*. What things was I supposed to think about? What are *things* anyway?

I can't say that I sat in the hall everyday but it sure felt like it. In fact, I longed to get away from the noisy classroom and be alone in the hall. Out in the hallway I could actually hear the lesson going on in the classroom. The distance made all the madness of the classroom less assaulting. No one poked me, or threw things. I didn't have to try to listen to the teacher when other children were constantly talking.

When they were talking I couldn't hear anything but noise. Just noise—all around me.

"Shut up!" I screamed holding my ears. "I can't hear."

"Jeannie, out in the hallway!" Ms. Montouri pointed toward the door to the desk that sat permanently out there waiting for me.

There was no point in staying in the room; she wasn't teaching us anything we didn't already know. Why would she teach an entire class to read? That is a waste of time, we knew that already. Then our times tables, really? This is kid stuff.

I raised my hand to answer the questions, I did. I waved my arms back and forth trying to keep my butt in the seat like she said I should. Still, she didn't call on me.

"Someone else—besides Jeannie. Does anyone else know the answer?"

When no one had the answer, I could no longer contain myself. I blurted it out.

"In the hallway."

I know, go think about *things*. Things are a problem.

"She was the last one in the school, and the last one out. She made the whole class wait for her every day." ~ Mom

School was a minefield. For starters, I was late every day because my alien leaders, the ones that dropped me off at my mother's house when I was born, didn't give her an instruction manual—and she was not a fast learner. We continued to struggle over what I would wear, and what I would eat, which was usually nothing. I didn't sleep well either so I was hard to wake in the morning, but much easier to wake than her.

School nights didn't mean much in my house; my parents liked to party. My brother and I stayed in their bedroom to go to sleep while aunts, uncles and friends played loud music, drank, smoked, and played cards.

I tried to sleep curled up in a ball under the covers cupping my hands over my ears trying desperately to drown out the noise. The smell of cigarette smoke and beer made me stomach sick and my eyes tear.

In the morning, navigating the sea of sleeping bodies sprawled out across the living room carpet surrounded by empty beer bottles, and half spilled over ashtrays brought on the vomit. Vomit brought on the screaming.

My screaming because even then I hated to vomit; although I should have been used to it, and my mother's screaming because now there was a mess to clean up. Now? There was a mess to begin with! Vomit was hard to get out of mustard-colored shag carpet.

Mornings sucked, school sucked, and we were late. At least I no longer needed to go see Mr. Hiler for a late pass; he was liar.

I was never in a rush; that much is true, but I certainly did not intentionally make the whole class late coming out of school every day—not intentionally.

The end of the school day was always the same.

"Pack your things, and line-up."

Line-up I had down. I was number three; Toni was number one, Laura was number two, then me, and Shayne was number four. Line-up: check. It was the pack your things part, the part that needed to be done before line-up that was the problem.

My desk was a wreck. The small space inside the metal-framed desk reserved for books was jam packed with my *things*. Papers were shoved inside, crumbed and torn. Pencils fell to the floor when I pulled on something I thought I needed to pack up, and was followed by an avalanche of debris that scattered across the floor making my head spin.

The mess, the chaos, and the lack of things having their own place made me feel sick. My brain ceased to work; I ceased to respond. I just stood there staring at the mess that I had no idea how to begin to clean up.

"We are not leaving until Jeannie cleans up this mess and packs her things."

I froze. There is that word again—things.

I made several attempts throughout the year to *pack-up my things*. All of them were wrong. I never arrived home with any of my textbooks, and couldn't do my homework. I spend the nights crying because my homework wasn't done, and the morning being screamed at because my homework wasn't done.

Going to school without my homework meant writing, *I must do my homework*, twenty times on the blackboard. I longed for the end of the day; longed to be out of the clutches of the classroom.

"Jeannie, pack up your things," the dreaded words seemed to echo throughout the room.

The whole class grumbled while I stood there staring blankly at my desk. They knew we were not leaving until I got my things together. The mother's waiting outside would be angry and grumbling that everyone always had to wait for me.

"If someone doesn't help Jeannie pack her things, we are going to stay here all day." Ms. Montouri said.

I didn't know what to pack.

Shayne, number four, rushed over to help. He helped me shove everything into my book bag, and slung it over his shoulder. Shayne wanted to go home.

From that day on Shayne helped me pack, or rather he packed my *things* for me. Actually he packed everything, and carried it because then it was too heavy and I couldn't lift it. I had to drag the book bag along, slowly.

When Shayne packed my book bag, I was able to do my homework. He packed the textbooks; I never did. The teacher told me to pack *my things*. The textbooks did not belong to me; they were not mine. They could *never be my things;* they were *their* things.

School *work* was easy, but navigating the school day without stepping on a landmine was not.

I tried to be a "good girl." A good girl listens to her teacher, and these instructions were clear.

"You're too skinny, drink this."

I stood there looking at the glass she held out in front of me with clear jellied slime with the yellow floating ball.

I tried to drink it; I did, but the minute the slime touched my lips everything inside my stomach found its way outside. It's a good thing I never ate breakfast or it would have been worse. I refused to drink it; I cried, I screamed, and I was brought to the office.

This time Grandma got the call, and she was furious. My teacher expected Mom to show up and instruct me to listen, to behave, and to drink her slime. She didn't expect Grandma.

If you thought a screaming, crying second grader could cause a commotion, you should have seen Grandma. My crying was nothing compared to what happened when she got there.

"How dare you!" Her voice was loud and filled the whole office. She walked past me sitting on the chair against the wall, past the startled school secretary, and went right for the woman with the witch's shoes and evil potion.

I've seen grandma mad before. Whenever my father would snatch the meatballs from her pan, everyone heard the *whomp*. Dad would come out of the kitchen rubbing the red welt grandma's wooden spoon left across his knuckles.

But now she was even angrier than that. I wondered if Ms. Montour was going to get whomped with that wooden spoon too.

"Raw eggs, are you crazy?" Grandma's voice grew even louder.

"She's too skinny. She needs more protein."

That's when the yelling really began. Grandma didn't like back talk.

I tried to listen but the room felt like it started spinning. All the words jumbled together so I couldn't understand them. I covered my ears, closed my eyes, pulled my knees to my chest, and rocked back and forth on the chair until it stopped.

"Come on." Grandma took my hand from my ears, "let's go home."

I didn't look at anyone when we left; I only followed grandma out of the building. I don't know what she said to Ms. Montouri that day, but she never tried to make me drink raw eggs again.

"You didn't like school, so you made your own." ~ Mom

Some autistic children line up cars, arrange their toys, books, and coin collections. I did all these things too. I methodically ordered my baseball card collection, and carefully arranged the stamp collection I started in the fourth grade. For me arranging things, making order out of chaos, was the most important part of playing; it was the part that brought me the most joy.

Playing school was one of my favorite things to do, which is odd considering the real thing was a nightmare. Maybe I longed for the idea of learning, for knowledge, for once again being smart. I loved facts, memorizing them quickly for instant recall when the teacher needed correcting.

"Don't correct your teacher in front of the class," mother said.

"Why?"

If she didn't need so much correcting I would have done it

less. I didn't understand why it was necessary for math problems to be long and drawn out. If she didn't know the answer, why didn't she just ask me? I knew it.

School was an endless struggle of confusing instructions. They wanted me to know the answer, but didn't want me to tell them what it was. They wanted me to raise my hand to be called on before answering, but then they didn't call on me. Instead they asked someone else who clearly didn't know the answer, *and* was not raising their hand.

All of it made no sense; my school was better. There were rules, they were clear, and had to be followed. In my school I was the teacher—always.

I spent hours setting the tables and chairs just right, arranging them so my students could see the chalk board. I collected textbooks, papers, pencils, crayons, chalk, and erasers. I gathered black and white notebooks for the class to practice writing their multiplication tables. Pretend things would not do; I needed real supplies.

In my classroom pencils were sharp, and children were quiet. I assigned classwork, and administered tests. I even assigned homework, and expected that my students/friends had it done the next day.

By the time my classroom was finished and ready to *play* my friends had run off. I remember arranging a perfect classroom in Cindy's house, in the porch room right by the door to the terrace. I was content arranging the items we needed, and had no any idea how long it had been since Cindy left to play dress-up in her room.

I liked *playing* school, but apparently it wasn't fun for anyone else. No one would play with me; they didn't want to do my homework assignments. I couldn't imagine why.

I suppose I should have been upset by this, I should have

been lonely, but in reality I was pretty content playing alone—setting up my classroom, *my things.*

I was creating on orderly, quieter, better version of school. Since real school had rules that I could not understand, I made my own.

Chapter Five: The Insta-Vomit Kid

It wasn't only the slime of raw eggs that produced insta-vomit. It was anything slimy that went into my mouth. If I didn't like the texture, taste, or more importantly, the smell of it—vomit was instantaneous.

To me that was my proof that I did not decide on my own what I could, or would eat. My sensitive palate decided for me.

A few days ago, my family and I ordered Chinese food. As I sat there with my husband and three boys, I reached for a spring roll. I like egg rolls, but the restaurant only had shrimp, and I can't eat shrimp.

The one bite I took of my spring roll sent me scrambling for a napkin and trying to make it to the bathroom. The inside was warm, and slimy. It felt like wet, mush in my mouth.

I can't eat food that is wet, or placed on a wet plate. If you are going to ask me to eat on a freshly rinsed plate, dry it first!

The instant need to expel the mush from my mouth was overwhelming. At 38 years old, I almost spit the food out of my mouth onto the table. Unfortunately, as a child, I *did* spit it right out. It was that or spew everything I'd eaten wherever I stood. I was a joy to eat with.

You'd think my mother would have stopped trying to force me to eat. Thank God for the dog. I slipped my food under the table when my mother's back was turned.

There were very few things I would eat. I spent an entire year only eating peanut butter sandwiches. No jelly, no crust, and the bread had to be fresh. If it was even a few days old (fresh by others' standards) I would not eat it. It lost its fresh bread smell.

I pulled each slice of bread out of the bag and pressed it against my nose to taking deep breaths, inhaling the smell of freshness. It didn't take me long to figure out that I only liked the smell of Wonder Bread. If it wasn't Wonder, I would not eat it. There was no fooling me either, I could tell the difference.

Thinking back now I see how Grandma's eating habits were very similar in nature to my own. She too would eat the same thing, at the same time, day in and day out. Every so often the routine started over with a new favorite food. I wish I could say this is something that lessened with age but it did not.

Today I am very much the same as I was then. I eat many more items because I cook them myself and control what goes in the pot, but I routinely eat the same things over and over again.

Grandma and I spent many years having lunch together. For months we ate lettuce and tomato with cottage cheese and salt at the same time every day, just before Grandma's stories came on television. Grandma watched *All My Children* every day.

"I have to be home for my stories," she said. Whatever we were doing ended, and we zipped home, making sure there was enough time to make lunch and sit down before it started.

When we arrived home Grandma peeled the tomatoes (no skin on fruits or vegetables—ever). She chopped the lettuce into small bite-size pieces, and pulled the Breakstone's Cottage Cheese out of the refrigerator. We could only eat Breakstone's, no other brand, and only whole milk.

When she tired of salad for lunch, we moved on to "one-eyed eggs."

One-eyed eggs were what Grandma called them. She took a slice of Wonder bread, pinched out a small hole in the middle, big enough for an egg yolk, and then pan fried the bread in butter to toast it lightly. She separated an egg, discarding the slimy whites, and gently placed the yolk in the center of the bread. It cooked for a few minutes, and then was flipped over with a spatula.

When it was finished I could cut pieces of the bread and dunk them in the center just like a sunny-side-up egg but without ever having to touch the whites, or pick the toast up with my hands.

I'm not sure if this was an actual recipe or Grandma just finding a way for me to eat the toast and eggs. I never minded the yolk, I liked to dip my toast but if my toast even accidentally touched any slime, and it touched my mouth—you guessed it—insta-vomit.

Food textures were not the only thing that sparked the appearance of the insta-vomit kid. Smells were even worse—enter the *Super-Sniffer*.

I smell things no one else can; even a faint remnant of odor in the air is registered by my super-sniffer.

I suppose it may have been easier to steer clear of smells that turned my stomach if I didn't need to smell everything before I ate it, and I mean everything.

Did you know that our sense of taste is based 80% in our

sense of smell?

I'm not surprised. For me I think it is even higher than that. I can quite literally taste what I smell. I will know exactly how something will taste just by sniffing it.

Many times I can pick out the individual ingredients used in the food—even if only in small amounts, the things that no one else seems to notice. In my house this is my super-power because I can re-create recipes from our favorite restaurants.

It is not surprising to me that smells produced the reaction they did. Have you ever tasted motor oil, body odor, or dirty socks? How about a dirty subway station, restroom, or bus exhaust? Rotten fish market? You get the idea. Any of these smells bring on the insta-vomit.

Some smells are so bad that they make me feel like I can't breathe. Aerosol sprays get stuck in my throat. Ammonia, bleach, pine-sol, and most air fresheners are intolerable—and perfumes are the worst!

There is a very real reason I only use things (lotions etc.) that smell like foods I like. Berry deodorant, fruit scented candles—who wants to taste lavender or lilies all day?

Growing up, I smelled all my food before I ate it, repeatedly, like sniffing the bread over and over again. This was partially to ensure I would be able to tolerate the food, but was also a stimming behavior.

Stimming is short for self-stimulatory behavior, sometimes called stereotypic behavior. Stimming refers to behaviors like hand flapping, rocking back and forth, and spinning. It is a way for autistic people to adapt to the sensory stimuli around them.

Stimming can occur when the autistic child or adult is happy, sad, overstimulated, or anxious. Foot flapping, pencil tapping, hair twirling, spinning round and round, smelling objects or people in some cases, and rubbing skin are all examples of stimming behaviors. They are meant to be calming actions which help regulate the overwhelming sensory input that the autistic person is experiencing, or to introduce sensory stimuli.

For me, smelling something good has a calming effect, it feels good. I can spend hours sniffing candles, or opening and closing the bottle of cucumber melon lotion.

Smelling foods was the same way. Breathing in the bread made me calmer. The more anxious I was, the more things I sniffed. Crowds of people made me anxious, and eating with strangers made me want to run and hide. If I couldn't get away, which was often the case, I needed to find something to smell.

Smelling food was a given, but if you added stress to the mix, it became worse.

My father finally grew tired of my embarrassing behavior. Every time he took me somewhere I refused to eat unless I smelled it first, which didn't guarantee I would eat it, and I sure was not going to *try* it. More often than not I wrinkled my nose, turned away, and pronounced, "I'm not eating that!"

I wasn't trying to be difficult, or rude. I didn't even comprehend those ideas. I had no idea that my behaviors could hurt someone's feeling, why would it? My intention was never to make anyone feel bad. It had nothing to do them; it was just that stinky food.

Every Christmas Eve my parents packed us in the car to Aunt Jenny and Uncle Eddie's house for dinner. Uncle Eddie was my grandfather's youngest brother. It was a short car ride; he only lived seven blocks from our house.

"You are going to eat whatever Aunt Jenny gives you," my father announced on our way there. "Do you understand me?"

I said nothing, but the ball that was bouncing around inside of my belly got bigger. There were often many stinky things on the table like artichoke hearts. What if she gives me artichoke hearts? If I don't eat them Dad will be mad.

Aunt Jenny's table was set with a red table cloth, fine white china trimmed in gold with matching golden utensils. Napkins the color of Christmas spruce were rolled inside golden leaved holders. Ivory candles rose from holy leaves in the center of the table.

The kids' table was set up in the center of the living room in front of the Christmas tree. The plastic table cloth had pictures of Santa, reindeers, and elves. There was an assortment of candies in small bowls in the center. The plates were paper, and the utensils plastic.

I never liked sitting at the kids' table. Not because I didn't like the table, but because I would have to sit with the other kids. Kids I did not recognize, even though they always seemed to know me. "Cousins," is what my grandmother called them, but to me they were strangers. I preferred to sit at the grown-up table.

The strange cousins ran around screeching and laughing as they went by while I sat near the tree worrying about when it would be time for dinner. This time I wanted to sit at the kids' table.

My father had me sit right next to him, something he never insisted upon. A heaping load of steaming lasagna was slid onto my plate. Sauce oozed down the sides of the pasta, cheesy strings of mozzarella hung off the sides of the plate. I was able to breathe at last. I could eat that; I liked lasagna.

After waiting for my lasagna to cool down I scooped some up with my fork, brought it to my nose and took a deep breath—

breathing in the smells of fresh basil, tomatoes, cheese—

It felt like an explosion. My breath caught in my throat, tears filled my eyes. My hand stung. The fork flew through the air, across the table, and landed with a resounding clank splattering sauce on the table.

"Joseph! What the hell is wrong with you?" Grandma yelled.

"She is going to eat whatever is put in front of her," he said.

My chest quivered with each sob that started coming out of my mouth. The table burst into shouts and commotion.

"Joe, calm down," Aunt Jenny said, "it's all right, she doesn't have to eat it."

But it wasn't all right, it was never all right again. From that night on, every time I smelled my food before eating, which was every time I ate, in front of my father he smacked the food out of my hands yelling, "Just eat it!"

The more he tried to smack the habit of smelling my food out of me, the more I needed to smell it. Eventually, I became immune to the smacks.

Chapter Six: Grasping for Control

The more life spun out of my control, the more I tried to control it. Or at least, control some parts of it—like handwriting. I physically had control over my own handwriting, so I exerted it.

Homework took hours. Hours of being yelled at to hurry up and get finished. Hours of erasing letters and starting over. Hours of sitting on the kitchen chair cross-legged rocking back and forth to drown out the crazy world around me.

I became obsessive about my writing. It had to be perfect. Every letter and every line had to be perfect. If I didn't like the look of the letter on the page, if it slanted slightly in the wrong direction I erased it, and started again.

Of course, the letters were never perfect enough. Sometimes they went under the line, and I had to do it again. Sometimes they were of different heights and not evenly spaced across the page. That would cause me to do the entire page over, not just erase and re-write one letter or word.

The contents of the sentences were of little importance.

They didn't have to make much sense at all, in fact, I often did not care what the words *said*, just that each letter be perfectly constructed.

I began stuttering and mispronouncing words when I was excited, upset, nervous, or stressed. I couldn't seem to get the correct words out of my mouth. Formulating blended letters became more difficult, not easier, with time.

The school said I was putting too much pressure on myself. The rocking back and forth while doing my homework was just what I did to concentrate. They were concerned about my speech, and so speech therapy began.

I liked going to speech, it got me out of my classroom every day. I had no problem working one-on-one with the teacher. After several years of speech, they proudly announced that my speech was improved—fixed, but that was only because there was no stress involved with sitting with one teacher and practicing the sounds of letters. That was a relaxing environment; it did not improve my speech outside that small classroom. Outside the classroom, I still stuttered and struggled to make my mouth formulate the correct sounds, and make my brain say the right words.

The efforts to fix me or smack the behaviors out of me met colossal failure. The constant stress triggered *nervous tics*. At least that is the name that was given for my blinking, squinting, nose wrinkling, mouth stretching, hand flapping, and foot tapping.

"She's just stressed out by the homework," the doctor said. "It's nothing to worry about. Just have her do only as much homework as she wants to. Then the tics will get better."

No more homework for me! The doctor said, "*Only do as much homework as she wants to*," and I heard him! After that if I wanted to do the homework, I did. If I didn't want to do it, I didn't. But—the tics did not stop.

I squeezed my eyes shut tightly and wiggled my nose after opening them. I opened my mouth stretching my jaw open as far as it could go. These movements were always in the same order. For this series of nonsensical body movements, there was no explanation.

When I started blinking all the time, the doctor thought I should have my eyes checked. I needed to close my eyes anytime I walked outside, anytime I walked inside, and anytime the lighting changed.

The bright light outside in the mornings caused me to keep my eyes shut tight even if I was walking. Opening my eyes was painful. It didn't matter that I walked into the light pole, fell down the curb into the street, or tumbled over piles of snow because I was not watching where I was going. I could not see where I was going, even if I did open my eyes.

The eye doctor could find no reason for my blinking, or squinting, or holding my eyes shut in the daylight. My vision was perfect; at least that is what his tests said. His diagnosis: I was allergic to the sunlight, and the florescent lights, and to the bright light bulbs.

I walked out of the eye doctor the proud owner of pearl framed, prescription tinted glasses. They made me look like a cross between a Martian and a bug. The *tint* was to protect my eyes from the light, and prescription lenses were precautionary. Just in case I did need to be able to see a little bit better. Those glasses made it worse. I could not see through the black tint, and they made the world fuzzy—even in the shade.

My sensitivity/allergy was attributed to my pale blue eyes. He said my eyes could not handle the bright lights because they were so light themselves. I suppose my blue eyes caused me to hear the buzzing in the light bulbs too?

Many of my strange behaviors were explained away. Rubbing my face on the dog, incessantly smelling the bubble gum, and sticking my head in the fence all had explanations.

Grandma bred German Shepherds. She loved dogs; she liked dogs more than people. I don't blame her. When I was in the first grade Grandma let me choose one of the puppies for my own. I named her Mindy. Had she been a he, I am sure his name would have been Mork since I really liked watching Mork and Mindy on television. I imagined that I too must be from Ork, another planet.

Mindy followed me wherever I went, maybe because she knew that food was coming her way. I slipped her food under the table, and sat with her on the stairs sharing my pretzels. "One bite for Mindy, one bite for Jeannie." I often referred to myself in the third person.

Mindy was my protector, and my comforter. When my parents fought, which was often, she stayed by my side. When dishes flew across the room slamming against the wall while my brother and I slept nearby, Mindy stood guard over us.

When I was particularly nervous or upset I used her as a pillow. She was soft, her fur was silken. I rubbed my face back and forth across her back. If I was sitting up I held onto her, and rocked back and forth while rubbing my hands up and down the tuft of fur under her neck.

Some thought my behavior was odd, but Grandma thought it was normal.

"I used to the do the same thing when I was a little girl," she said.I loved to sniff bubble gum, especially watermelon flavored gum.

Grandpa owned a vending machine route—gumballs. Every

night he sat in his golden-yellow arm chair in the parlor, which sat next to Grandma's pink one, and put his capsules together. The machines that contained gumballs were easy to fill—just open the box and pour them into the top of the machine. But the plastic capsules that contained small toys and other prizes were not as easy. The capsules needed to be assembled.

I sat with Grandpa for hours in the evening time. The two of us filled the bottom of the capsule with a prize, snapped on the top, and tossed the finished ones into a big box. The nightly routine and repetitive motion was comforting. It gave me something to do, and I got to help Grandpa. Besides, it was always more peaceful upstairs in their apartment than downstairs in mine.

The gumballs were kept in the garage. I followed Grandpa through the driveway and into the backyard where he flung open the rolling garage door. There were boxes stacked high to the ceilings filled with toy prizes, hard candies, and gumballs. I searched out the green ones.

The green gumballs were watermelon flavor. I didn't want to chew them; I only wanted to smell them. I loved the smell of watermelon gum.

"Your grandfather didn't let you chew the gum," my mother said, "that's why you always stood there smelling them."

She was partially right. He wouldn't allow me to sit around all day chewing gum, not with my awful teeth. He was sure that if I took a bite into that hard coated gumball my teeth would shatter. He may have been right too.

I've always had awful teeth. *Milk teeth,* my mother always called them, although I don't know what that means. The dentist said I had soft enamel. By the time I was four years old, I knew my dentist by name.

I had many teeth that had to be extracted probably due to a number of factors. I refused to give up my bottle, sleeping with it until I was over three years old, and the milk, I'm told, rotted my teeth. I had soft enamel—and bad oral hygiene. Brushing regularity was an all-out war. I hated the feel of the toothbrush on my gums, and the taste of the toothpaste made me gag. None of these reasons were why I sniffed the bubblegum then, or the reason I love to sit here and just smell fruity candy and gums (but not chew on them) now.

Some of the things that I did just could not be explained away; the explanations made no sense.

"You just wanted to see the red fire truck" ~Mom

My husband and I were driving home from a doctor's appointment last week when a fire engine roared past the van. I gritted my teeth, squeezed my eyes closed, and put my fingers in my ears. The sound of that siren scratched my brain and made my teeth hurt.

When the engine was far enough down the road that the sound was bearable, I unclogged my ears and watched it roll out of sight. That's when I realized that there was no way I was intentionally trying to make the fire truck come to our house.

I have a long list of strange things that I used to do as a child. Sitting very close to the top of the list is getting my head stuck in the fence.

We lived in a two-story, two-family house in Brooklyn. My grandparents lived on the second floor, rented the first floor, and we lived in the basement apartment. A tall maple tree stood in our front yard. My grandmother's second-floor porch was enclosed by a black wrought-iron fence.

I often played out on Grandma's porch, either while she was

inside the small attached room knitting, or sitting outside sipping coffee. I don't know what made me stick my head between the bars of the fence. Maybe there was something interesting in the front yard that I could only see by sticking my head as far through the iron fence as I could.

I wasn't a baby, a toddler, or even a preschooler; I was already in elementary school. My head should not have even fit through the bars.

Grandma heard my screams and came running out onto the porch. I had managed to get my head through the fence, but I couldn't get it back out. I was stuck, and stuck good. She called my grandfather, and neither of them could dislodge my head. My ears were in the way. They called the fire department.

I heard the roar of the sirens blazing down 65th street, and could see them stop to make the turn onto 19th Avenue from my space in the fence. The neighbors came out of their houses to see what all the commotion was about. Doors opened, and neighbors walked out onto their terraces to watch the firemen dismount from their truck. Two men entered the front door to come upstairs, while the others waited out front.

When they came out onto the porch, one of the fire fighters knelt down next me. I saw the metal cutter in his hand.

"What are you doing? I asked.

"I'm going to get you out."

"How?"

"I'm going to cut the fence—"

"Why?" I said whipping my head around to look at him. "Don't do that!" To his amazement I was free, and walked back into my grandparent's apartment.

Soon the neighbors came out only periodically when the firemen arrived. Instead of worrying there might be a fire, they assumed Jeannie was stuck *again*.

Chapter Seven: My One Friend; My Only Friend

"Children aren't coloring books. You don't get to fill them with your favorite colors." —Khaled Hosseini

It would have been easier if others could have colored me in with precise, conforming colors; easier for them, that is. Trying to color me in was like coloring with melting crayons. You couldn't press too hard without winding up with a puddle of something warped and mushy. My colors ran all over the page, poured out of the lines and meshed together to form colors no one had yet recognized. I was different–unique, bold, strong, smart, and hard-headed. I was simply me.

Efforts to fix me, or demand I conform to the normal world around me only resulted in my retreat. I retreated into my own world–further into the depths of my foggy existence. It is surprising to me how much I can recall, and more surprising still, how much I cannot.

I recall things about myself, situations, and places, but recall very few people. I don't remember much contact with friends or family. They always just seem to be on the outside of my memory, on the fringes, fuzzy and faded out.

Looking back on my early years, and first school experiences, I realize that no one truly understood me. The standing assumption was that all my difficulty was the result of a stubborn mind.

In reality that is not far from the truth. My autistic brain is stubborn, unyielding, and immovable. My thought processes were difficult to change at best and impossible at worst. I simply do not possess the flexibility of mind to tolerate changes in routines, or abrupt changes in activities.

I did not simply want to do things my way; I could not do it any other way. Nor did I comprehend that there was another way to do things, or another way of being. I lived in simple oblivion–confusing oblivion, but oblivion all the same.

I didn't understand the odd stares, or know to feel left out when children didn't play with me. I was simply happy playing in my own world without anyone intruding or trying to change the way the game was played. It never occurred to me to feel lonely. It never occurred to me that I was different, or that the difference pushed others away.

I did have friends when I was young; although they were always built-in friends, friends that were in my life as a result of other situations. I played with the children of my mother's friends, or the children that lived on our block. They were inserted into my life, always present, and so just a natural part of my being.

Making friends outside of my world was a completely different story. Those friends, friends made in school, or girl scouts, or dance class didn't exist. I did not maintain or cultivate any of those friendships. In fact, I don't remember having any of those types of friendships during this period in my life. I had no need for them–no need for more than one friend at a time. In fact, I could not tolerate more than one friend at a time—ever.

If I could not play with my friend alone, or if other children showed up, I simply left if I could. Otherwise, I would go play in a corner by myself. These are the times that I began to feel confused and alone. Never could I relate to, or understand the need, to play in groups.

Groups are overwhelming. There are too many things to focus on, too many people to listen to at one time, and too many people to ensure they are playing correctly. It's exhausting.

I've always only had one friend at time; one person to confide in, and share my life with. This is as true today as it was when I was four years old. One friend was all I ever needed, and I discarded the rest.

Friends are time-consuming, dramatic, and exhausting. They take energy, and work. I have never been able to maintain casual relationships, acquaintances, or contacts. They fade quickly into the background like insignificant chit-chat.

My choice of friend is total; all or nothing. I am an all-the-way, all-the-time friend, or nothing at all. My friend will be totally immersed in my life, or completely cut-off.

Don't fret over the lonely child with only one friend; I was not lonely. I had a friend who was always there with me, getting in trouble alongside me, and sharing the craziness life threw at us. I didn't choose her, or her me–our mothers were friends. Both our mothers yelled, both our fathers drank–we were a perfect match; Vanessa and I.

Autistic children often show no real fears of danger despite obvious risks of harm.

This may be easy to spot in a young child who bolts for the street at a moment's notice, or plunges into water with no fear of its depth without being able to swim. But what does it look like in an older child, one on the cusp of adolescence?

"Nannie" is what we call my grandmother on my mother's side. I've never called her grandma; she is Nannie, my *other* grandmother.

Nannie worked in amusement parks for as long as I can remember; Rockaway Amusement Park, Rye Playland, and Crossbay Amusement Park. Crossbay Amusement Park was a small kiddie park on Crossbay Boulevard in Howard Beach. During the summer when I was 12 years old, Nannie got me and Vanessa jobs working with her at the amusement park.

We learned how to operate the kiddie rides, strap in the children, and watch over them as they rode. I manned the motorcycles and Vanessa the boats. The sounds from the honking horns and dinging bells often left my head spinning.

The park closed at 10 p.m., and the last bus into Broad Channel ran at 11:00 p.m. We often got off of work and took the bus into Broad Channel with Nannie, where my uncle Alan met us and drove us on to her house in Rockaway Beach. On nights when Nannie was not working Vanessa and I took the bus into Broad Channel alone to meet my uncle.

One night after we closed down the rides we hung around the park instead of heading straight for the bus stop. Before we realized the time, eleven o'clock had come and gone, and we missed the last bus running over the bridge. There were no payphones on the corner, and no cellphones in our pockets enabling us to call for a ride, and we needed to get over that bridge. But first, we needed to get to the bridge.

With absolutely no concept of fear, we devised a plan—we would walk. I didn't say it was a good plan. When a motorcyclist stopped to ask us if we needed a ride, we were ecstatic. I suppose two young girls walking down a deserted street heading for a bridge looked like they needed a ride somewhere. The problem was that we both could not fit on the back of the bike, and even if we could that was dangerous.

I didn't want to leave Vanessa alone, but needed to get to the entrance of the bridge so we can start walking over it. We decided that I would go first, and Vanessa would stay hidden behind a bush. The man could drop me off by the entrance of the bridge, where I could wait, and then return for her.

Thankfully neither one of us were killed or kidnapped, and we were brought safely to the entrance of the bridge—the vehicle entrance. There was a walking path. A wire fence separated the road from the path. The only route to the walkway from where we were was over the fence. With no thought whatsoever the two of us began to climb the fence on the bridge.

We made it only half way up when we were blinded by headlights and deafened by the sound of a horn.

"What are you doing? Get down from there; you want to get yourselves killed?" My uncle was out of his car and pulling us down off of the fence before I realized who was yelling at us. I guess he figured when we failed to get off the last bus he'd better go looking for us.

It never occurred to me to just wait at the amusement park, or that my uncle would come to pick us up. In my mind I had to get to the meeting place, to the bus stop, and that was what I was going to do. I was a fearless problem solver.

When I get it in my head to do something, it is set in stone, concrete, stuck, immovable.

Many children cannot perceive the dangers that lurk around them, the dangers that the real world poses. I often tell my own children why their actions were dangerous, and warn them of what could have happened. I can see the light bulb go on (most of the time) when they process what I say and perceive the danger in their actions. My light bulb failed to ever turn on.

I could not imagine that the motorcyclist picking up two hitchhiking young girls could be dangerous. I would not kidnap anyone, I was not thinking about running off with him, so why would he run off with me? I dismissed the lecture of danger; the fact that his intentions could have been any different than my own never crossed my mind.

I should have felt it was dangerous to roam the streets of Brooklyn in the middle of the night, but I felt no such thing. Vanessa and I often snuck out of our houses at nighttime and roamed around the neighborhood. When our parents found us missing in the morning we told them we left very early to go jogging. After all, joggers were out before the sun exercising, weren't they?

Our parents accepted this jogging excuse. Had they ever realized that we'd roamed around all night long? Mine were too lost, too wrapped up in their own world. I was fortunate to have a friend who came with me to roam the neighborhood in the middle of the night. The times when she could not, I roamed alone.

The more unbearable life at home became, the more I wandered through the streets at night time. I always had difficulty sleeping. I could not fall asleep, and if I did, screaming parents often woke me. The screaming that woke me in the night became frequent, nightly, and then constant.

They fought about money, mostly. My father's gambling problem was spinning out of control, and leaving him broke and angry. The more he gambled, the more he drank; the more he drank, the more he gambled. Holes punched in our walls were a common occurrence when he arrived home from the racetrack.

My mother was no picnic either. She tossed plates at him, smashing them against the walls. The lack of money meant a lack of partying; a lack of alcohol; a lack of drugs. I escaped into the fog, into the quiet, into the night, and I roamed. Just before my twelfth birthday I decided that I was running away.

I was not running away alone. Theresa lived two doors down and she was going to run away with me, and of course Vanessa was too. The plan was to take the N train into the city, change for the path train, and run away to Theresa's uncle's house in New Jersey. There we all could start new lives, and work in his pizzeria. We had a plan.

I slept at Vanessa's house that night, and at 4 a.m. we prepared to leave for our new life. We hadn't counted on her Dad being up getting ready to leave for work.

"Where are you two going?" he asked.

"Jogging," Vanessa said. "Can you give us some money so we can go eat breakfast when we are done?"

Our "jogging" habit had paid off. We were on our way, to meet Theresa at the 18th Avenue train station with train money in hand.

The three of us boarded the "N" train, and were hurled off toward the city. We didn't make it that far. At the 36th street train station Theresa came to her senses and decided she needed to go home. She had no reason to run away.

My mind was already made-up, I was running away. I could not turn back now. Theresa was two years older than me and was crucial to the plan. She had lined-up our new life. What was I going to do now?

Theresa suggested I go home too, but I refused, and Vanessa couldn't let me go alone. They couldn't change my mind; I couldn't change my mind. My mind was set, and I was going. The problem was, going where?

The summers working in the amusement park in Howard Beach taught us how to take the buses to the Rockaways. Vanessa and I made our way to Nannie's house on the trains, and buses. I would have run away to Grandma's house, the one who understood me, but she was only one flight of stairs away. It was too close; I needed to get further away from the fighting, further away from the noise, further away from the madness.

By the time we arrived at Nannie's house they were expecting us, and my parents were on their way. I tried to get away; I tried to climb out a second story bedroom window onto a nearby roof. There was no escape, nowhere to run, my parents were coming, and they were going to take me back home.

I waited for it, the slaps—but this time they didn't come. My father yelled, demanding to know why I'd run away. I thought the answer was in the question. I thought it had been obvious. All his words blended into one another the further I retreated inside myself, until I didn't hear him anymore at all. I had completely shut down.

I sat in my room "staring into space," his words, for hours.

"It's like talking to a brick wall," he said before finally storming off into the other room.

When Vanessa's parents asked why she ran away she said, "I couldn't let Jeannie run away alone." Vanessa was grounded for a month.

I didn't get grounded—ever. My mother said keeping me inside with her was only punishing herself. God forbid I intrude on her world.

Chapter Eight: Acting the Part

By the time I was nearing the end of elementary school, I had learned how to live by a script. I learned by watching television, by looking at magazines, and by reading books. In the fourth grade, I learned about having my period by reading *Are you there God? It's me, Margaret*, by Judy Blume. I read, and re-read that book many times during the fourth and fifth grades. Margaret became one of my best friends.

I loved my books; all my friends lived in there! My friends often lived inside my books, and the television set. I imagined interactions with the characters, and tried to think of what *they* would say in different situations. Every interaction was re-played out in my head before it happened—if I could foresee an event.

For instance if I were to contemplate asking a friend to come over to our house to play, I would have the conversation over and over again in my head before approaching the girl. Many times my own words sounded stupid when I played them and I decided not to offer an invite.

After an interaction, I'd replay the scene hundreds of times judging if I sounded "stupid". I imagined what would have happened if I said this or that, often berating myself for saying the wrong thing. My voice, my words were usually wrong so I tried to become other people, to take on other personas.

I tried to be the beautiful model in the picture hanging on the wall of the hair salon. If I could be her then all the girls would want to be my friend. This particular model had extremely short hair, shaved in the back with longer waves on top. The kind of hair you can only get from having professional stylists work on it for hours before a photo shoot, which is something I failed to understand at the time.

I wanted to be her, I wanted that haircut, and so my mother allowed the hairdresser to cut my hair short—very short.

I didn't look like the model, in fact, I looked like a boy! I of course was unaware of this fact until I went to school the next day.

In the fourth grade a boy's haircut does not a popular girl make, so I had my ears pierced. For sure now with pretty studded earrings I could not look like a boy, but at school my pretty ears did nothing to detract from my head.

Pretending to be someone else became an obsession. I watched my grandmother's stories (soap operas) and picked out characters to emulate—definitely not the best role models. When I found out that they were just actors and actresses playing a part, with a script, I knew I needed to be an actress. I could do a script, and I was already used to dancing on stage so this would be a cinch.

Scripts were just like dance routines, they were choreographed for you and as long as you follow the script you were doing it right.

Anything I want to do, I want to do perfectly. People often tell me that practice makes perfect, but that is not true. Perfect practice makes perfect. If you routinely practice something the wrong way, you will always do it that way. The only way to achieve perfection is to practice perfectly. I afforded myself no room for error—ever.

I knew nothing about acting so the logical thing to do was to go to acting school. Vanessa and I convinced our mothers to sign us up for an acting school in Manhattan.

There was an audition to be accepted. We created our own Toys-R-Us commercial to include acting, dancing, and singing—it was mostly dancing and singing. We practiced until we had every step and every word down perfectly.

I remember riding the train to the city, excited that I was going to be an actress. The possibility of this not happening never crossed my mind.

The audition went well and we were accepted. Vanessa and I spent many hours learning how to act, and for the most part it was an exciting and fun experience. The problem happened when one day we were given no scripts—improvisation.

Our assignment was to perform a simple silent skit, no words, and no props of any kind. I felt the ball bouncing around in my stomach, the tears welling up in my eyes. My insides felt like they were shaking; panic was setting in.

I could not do it—I wound up acting out the task of making macaroni and cheese in my kitchen. It was the disaster that ending my acting school career.

Although I continued to try to adopt different personas, looking for a person that I could be, I was not very good at the task. I was able to adopt a precious few, but had tremendous difficulty switching between them, deviating from the carefully constructed script. Not all personas work in every situation.

I was a terrible actress. Who needed improvisation anyway? At least I still had my dancing.

I struggled to hold on to that part of me, the one thing that was mine, my identity as a dancer. I knew I was good at it, and I practiced and obsessed about its perfection.

Junior High School was approaching and I was hoping to go to Mark Twain, a Junior High School in Coney Island. It was a school for gifted students requiring an entrance (academic) exams, interview, and talent audition. In addition to excellent academics, students needed to demonstrate a talent in one or more areas of the arts.

Despite my rarely doing homework, and spending many of my days banished to the hallways, academically, I remained at the top of my class. Thanks to my hyperlexia, by the third grade I had an eighth grade reading level, and by the fifth grade, a twelve grade reading level.

I breezed through the entrance exams. Step one: top grades, and high passing scores on the entrance exam; check.

Step two consisted of choosing two talents; that was tough. Dancing was a given, but I played no musical instruments, was not confident in my singing ability, and my drawing and painting was mediocre at best. That left acting, so acting it was. I had training and experience on stage, and preparing a monologue was right up my alley—no interaction with anyone else needed.

The dance audition was first. I chose a solo piece I'd recently performed from Swan Lake—on pointe. Every step was in tune, every movement graceful, and every pirouette perfect. I nailed it, and I knew it. Smiling judges applauded; I was beaming.

"Now we are going to play a random selection of music for your freestyle dancing. Just do whatever comes naturally," one of the judges said.

What? My heart sank. I stood there staring at the panel of four judges, three female, and one male. No one told me, I had nothing prepared, no plan, and no idea what to do. I stood there even after the music began.

"You can begin," a voice came from the table of judges, and so I did.

I began, at the beginning of my prepared ballet routine. I adjusted for the pace and the tempo of the music, which was something out of Flash dance, but that did not make my attempt at freestyle dancing any less ridiculous.

It wasn't until years later that I understood what was expected that day. That they wanted to see how I would move on a dance floor. When the music started to play, could I dance? Did I have any rhythm?

The rest of the day went by in a teary blur. My monologue was rushed; my face was flushed red from fretting over the dance scene that confounded me. The same unpleasant surprise awaited me at the end of my prepared piece. The instructions: "Pretend you are alone at a school dance."

I stared down at the polished wood floors, and paced back and forth watching myself turn red in the mirrors before sitting down in a chair against the wall.

I glanced up to see four sets of eyes on me. Twisting my hands in my lap I began to mumble, "I shouldn't have come here today; I want to go home."

The call for the entrance interview never came.

Chapter Nine: A Confusing Middle Ground

"Remember, Hope is a good thing, maybe the best of things, and no good thing ever dies." ~ Steven King

My hope was dying.

My fragile facade, the tattered house of cards I'd erected, came crashing down. My identity, the persona I became, the self I'd adopted, failed.

She didn't dance, she didn't twirl, she didn't shine—she faded.

Thrust out of the safety of elementary classes with no hope of specialized schooling, the confusing transition to a middle ground began.

People rushed around me in every direction. I was caught standing in the middle of a busy intersection that was the school hallway, but there was no traffic light, and no street signs to mark my way.

I was lost on the third floor again, I think. Or, did I get off the staircase on the second floor? I was sure my computer class was in this corner of the hall.

A paper plane made of white wide-ruled loose leaf paper hit me in the head sticking to my hair. That's when I felt the thump on my back and watched my book bag fly to the floor almost taking me with it.

I noticed the laughing before I saw the contents of my bag sprawled across the hallway. Papers were stepped on as dozens of kids tramped by, a sneaker hit my pen just as I was about to reach it launching it further into the sea of legs rushing past.

I scrambled across the floor to gather my books and haphazardly shoved them back into my bag.

The bell rang, and the traffic sped up, clearing most of the hall. Flushed and disoriented I stood up and looked around.

"She's lost again," a girl said shaking her head as she walked toward the entrance of the classroom at the end of the hall.

"What an idiot," another girl snickered before disappearing into the room.

Another bell rang—*great, late again.* I shuffled into the class behind the two girls, not knowing if that was the right room. I figured that if they knew I was lost they were probably in my class, although I was sure I hadn't seen them before. Besides, it wouldn't be the first time I'd burst into the wrong class room late.

Just the day before I ran into my social studies class, sat down, and took out my books only to realize that the room had become quiet and even the teacher was staring at me. "You don't belong in this class young lady," she said. *Dear God please let this be the right room this time.*

It didn't matter how many times I entered that building, I became lost every time. This new world of classes that changed locations every 45 minutes wreaked havoc on my school life.

I could not make it to school on time. I wandered the three long New York City blocks to school in the morning lost in my own thoughts. Each day I stopped at a small candy store on 17th avenue before school to buy two cowtails to eat on my way. It didn't matter the time, I had to stop.

I suppose it would not have been so bad if I was only late in the morning, but I wasn't. I was late to every single class. Either I could not pack my things quickly enough to make it to the next classroom on time, or I would get lost in the crowd and wind up in the wrong place wandering desperately trying to find my way.

I continually showed up to the wrong classrooms at the wrong times. Keeping my schedule straight, the locations of the classes, and the books needed for each subject was nearly an impossible task.

After a long humiliating day of school, I had nothing left—no brain power or discipline. There was no way in the world homework was getting done. I suspect that many autistic children have this difficulty. By the time they arrive home, school has sucked all the life out of them. This certainly was the case for me.

I was drained from trying to be where I needed to be, trying to keep up with my things, and that didn't even take into consideration the actual people around me. Junior High/Middle School dynamics differ greatly from elementary relations.

There were always cliques, but middle school made them more prevalent. The girls I was friends with as a child, mostly because of them being in the same class as me or friends of my mother's, now had no obligation to remain friends with the freak who could not remember where the computer class was after six months of school. Who wanted to be seen with the girl who was constantly scrambling after her things rolling down the halls?

Although I was able to execute a choreographed dance routine perfectly, I couldn't walk without tripping over my own feet. Gym class was always entertaining—for the other people in my class.

I remember trying to learn how to ride a bicycle when I was about 10 years old. I learned how to ride much later than the rest of the children on the block. I did all right when I rode the bikes with only back petal brakes, the ones that you stop peddling forward, and use your feet to go backwards in order to stop. I often crashed into poles, and flew over the Johnny pump on our block, but that was nothing compared to trying to ride a bike that employed hand brakes.

How did I manage to tip over sideways while riding and go splat onto the sidewalk? Or fly head first over the handle bars when depressing both the front and back breaks with my hands. I found it difficult to apply equal amounts of pressure with my left and right hands on the brakes simultaneously.

I would either squeeze the back brakes harder, or before the front, or worse, depress the front brakes first or with more pressure than the back sending me sailing over the front of the bike. Bicycle riding was hazardous to my health.

Have you ever heard the expression, "can't ride a bike and chew gum at the same time?" Well, that was me—literally. I literally cannot do it, not then, and certainly not today. Riding required my attention. I must use my legs to pedal and make sure that I use both hands at the same time to break. If you added chewing gum, eating candy, or talking of any sort I hit the floor.

When I was first dating my husband he wanted to go for a bike ride. He often liked to bike ride, roller blade, and do various outdoor physical activities—all of which ending in some interesting and embarrassing stories for me.

One day we decided that we were going to take a ride down by the water. My brother John came along. We rode alongside the water and down under the Verrazano Bridge.

"You had to see her. I watched her riding in front of me, then without stopping the bike started tipping over to the side until she was on the ground," my husband recalled during Thanksgiving dinner. "When I asked her what happened, she told me she had no idea. She was riding and then was on the ground."

That is exactly how it happened too. If you liked to laugh, I was interesting to be around.

Being interesting, hard headed, and independent worked in my favor. Since everyone usually laughed at the stupid things I did or got myself into, I became the class clown.

It didn't happen on purpose exactly. I had the habit of not being able to filter my thoughts before they flew out of my mouth. I wasn't trying to be funny on purpose, nor was I trying to be insulting or to make fun of other people. But come on, if the English teacher came in to teach in leather pants what did she expect?

My flying thoughts were either met with scorn and ridicule, usually by other girls, or giggles and high-fives that came from the boys in class. I developed a reputation for always saying what I thought, and not caring how other people felt about it. The problem was, I didn't understand why this was even something to notice. Didn't everyone say what they thought? Why would you say anything else?

I did not have to work hard for my grades for the most part. If I needed to learn something, and I was interested in it, all I had to do was read. If I read the book, the information was usually branded onto my brain. That comes in handy when it is test time.

In the lower grades as long as I was able to do well on tests my grades stayed up. That made sense to me. I took the test, passed (usually with a 100 percent) so I knew the work and should get an A right?

In the seventh grade I wound up in the principal's office often (are you noticing a pattern here?). This time it was because I was being accused of cheating on my math tests. I didn't like being accused of cheating, or lying—ever. Giving me "F's" on tests I had done well on was an injustice I was unable to bear.

My mother often had to come up to school because of my "cheating," and the yelling, screaming, and crying that followed. My behavior was "uncalled for and inappropriate" is what they said.

"Do you want her to take the test again?" my mother asked. That made me even angrier, why should I have to do the work twice just because they refused to believe that I knew how to do the work.

"Yes, but she must show all her work."

I never understood why the math teacher did problems the way he did. Why did he have to go through all those meaningless complicated steps just to get the answer, when he could have just asked me? I knew the answer, but I never knew how I'd come up with it. In fact, if I was made to "show my work," or forced to do the math problem in the way they taught it, I could not do it. I arrived at the incorrect answer every time.

Apparently being smarter than the teacher and getting the answers my own way was unacceptable. I failed Math class for the first time in my life. This taught me two things: being smart didn't matter, and grades mattered even less because they did not reflect what you knew or what you did not. They only reflected your ability to follow other people's ways of doing things, even if those ways make no sense. *That* was something I have never been able to do.

My greatest asset was my inability to fit in, my inability to conform, and my stubborn immobility. The inflexibility to change my mind once made up, immune to persuasion has made me strange— odd—different. This is one difference that I would never change; my immunity to peer pressure.

Peer pressure is another concept that I never could grasp. Doing things you knew were wrong just to fit in, or things you didn't want to do in order to what? Keep your friends? Look good?

The one thing no one could ever say about me, is that my friends made me do it. I never followed the crowd; I couldn't. I led, they followed, or I went alone.

No one was able to convince me do something I did not want to do; it simply was not possible. Once I decided, that decision was final, and forever. Everything was black and white, right or wrong, good or bad—no middle ground. If I'd judged something wrong; it was wrong, and nothing, no situation, no justification could make something wrong—right.

The key here though is when *I judged something*. My morality or idea of such was not swayed by other people, but also was not always in line with their idea of acceptable.

"There is only one sin. and that is theft... when you tell a lie, you steal someone's right to the truth." — Khaled Hosseini, The Kite Runner

Something as seemingly simple as social niceties to me was unacceptable behavior. Lying just to make someone feel good was not acceptable to me; in fact, I didn't even understand the concept. Why would someone do that? If I ask you a question, it is because I am truly expecting you to answer me—honestly.

It didn't take very long for my friends to figure out that if they really wanted to know how they looked in a certain pair of pants to ask me. But if they wanted to feel good about themselves, or to hear that their hair looked fine when it was really sticking up in the air and looked like a little surfer man should have been riding the waves, then, I was not the one to ask.

I didn't receive the manual. You know, the manual where these social rules were written—but it appeared that everyone else around me had. I often argued the reasoning for such stupidity. Why are you asking me a question that you don't really want the answer to? If you don't want an honest answer, then don't ask!

I would rather you tell me that I looked awful before I walked out of the house, than to lie to me. If I looked terrible I could possibly do something about it (if I cared at the moment that is), but if you lie then you take the opportunity to make things better from me. I simply could not understand the necessity of a little white lie. Lying was not something that ever came naturally.

Chapter Ten: Immune to Peer Pressure; Learning to Socialize

Immunity to peer pressure does not mean unimpressionable. How do children learn to socialize? How do they adapt to the changing dynamics of their social life as they grow older?

My friends could not change my mind once it was made up, but what made up my mind? I was impressed upon by books, television shows, family, and friends much like everyone else with one important difference—I never felt any pressure to fit in. The things that I decided to do needed to be my decision, and mine alone. I was never going to do something simply because you wanted me to.

"She has a mind of her own." ~Grandma

I suppose my grandmother was correct, but my mind was not always brilliant. It often had some real hair-brained ideas. Like the time Vanessa, my friend and partner in mischief, and I decided that it was ridiculous to have to reapply lipstick every day. We reasoned that since nail polish didn't wipe off of our nails, it shouldn't wipe off of our lips—right? If we polished our lips with pearly pink nail polish they would match our nails.

Before going to sleep that night we polished our nails, and yes—our lips. Do you know what happens when nail polish dries on your lips when you are sleeping? You wake up with dry, cracked, bleeding lips. They were far from the pretty pearly pink that we had envisioned.

To make matters worse the only way to remove the polish would have been to pick it off, piece by painful piece along with the skin on our lips. Unless—we used nail polish remover! That for sure would take it all off. It was not a good morning.

Although our lip painting fiasco was painful, for the most part it was harmless. Some other ideas we had, not so much.

My father often sent me around the corner to buy beer and cigarettes. It never occurred to me that children were not supposed to be allowed to purchase these items since this is always how it had been.

One day Vanessa and I decided we were going to hang-out and drink some beer together. We knew that we could purchase the beer and no one would ask if it was for my father or for us.

"How much do you think we should get?" she asked.

"A six-pack each?" I said. That was what our father's always drank, a six pack in front of the television. But we were not going to drink in front of the television; we were going to drink a few blocks over in an alleyway that ran behind a row of houses on 61st street.

We walked the four blocks from the store toting our six packs inside brown paper bags. When we arrived at the alleyway, we walked down the sloping drive and sat on the curb in front of a row of garages. It was already getting dark, and it was chilly.

We talked and laughed chugging down our cans of beer, which we both agreed tasted disgusting. The taste, however, faded the more cans we drank until we didn't notice the nasty taste at all. We laughed, fell over, and giggled some more.

"What are you kids doing back there?" a voice shouted from a nearby window.

"We better get out of here," Vanessa said, "Run!"

We ran up the sloped drive leaving a mess of beer cans, and crumbled bags of chips behind. We ran at least another block before stopping to laugh. We laughed so hard it became difficult to not pee our pants. We needed to get back to the house to use the bathroom, and quick.

The two of us walked up 20th avenue back toward my house. The thought never occurred to me that we could be in trouble, or that we shouldn't have been drinking beer. I spent my entire life emulating and adopting different personas to see which fit into different social situations. Hanging out with friends and drinking beer seemed a good "fit".

The two of us stumbled to 64th street laughing before Vanessa got sick. We almost made it; we were only a block from my house. We had drank those beers down so quickly that we had no idea what was coming; no idea that alcohol takes about 30 minutes to work its way through your system. I suppose that 30 minutes had passed.

Vanessa *borrowed* her Aunt's sweater before leaving her house earlier that day. When I say borrowed, I mean she borrowed it out of her closet without asking her first. Our heads were spinning so we sat down on a small brick wall outside a storefront. Vanessa wound up with her head in the bushes as more beer expelled itself from her stomach.

Laughter had turned to crying. "Kim's sweater!" Vanessa said with tears rolling down her face. "She's going to kill me."

"We need to get back home, and then we'll wash it," I said.

"No, she'll know I borrowed it. She'll kill me. I have to get rid of it. Let's throw it away."

The night had turned cold but with a six-pack of beer in each of us we didn't feel the cold. In fact we didn't feel much of anything. When Vanessa borrowed that sweater that morning, she had no way of knowing it would wind up in the 20th avenue sewer covered in beer induced vomit by the end of the night.

Yes—that was what we were worried about. Not being in trouble for drinking beer, that was normal, but ruining a perfectly good sweater. Instead of washing it, our idea was to get rid of it by throwing it in the sewer. Can you see we were not thinking too clearly?

I had to run up the block to get my mother. I never worried about her being mad, in fact, that thought never crossed my mind. Why would she be made at me for drinking beer? They drank beer every day; it wasn't illegal. I guess the fact that I was not yet thirteen years old never factored itself into my legal vs. illegal equation at the time. I considered the small detail of alcohol being legal without applying it properly to the whole picture (under-age drinking).

Vanessa was too sick for me to help her back to my house alone; at least my vomit waited until I was back at home.

I would like to report that it was the first and last time I deemed drinking with friends socially acceptable behavior, but that would be a lie. Maybe it was a lack of consequences that instilled the idea that alcohol was a good social tool to use. Maybe it was something that I was so familiar with because of my home life that it provided a comfort of sorts. That coupled with the numbing effect it had on my senses made it the tool of choice for many years to come. Instead of being in a constant sensory overload, alcohol offered an interesting quiet, a dulling of my super-senses.

My junior high school/middle school years rushed by in a blur. I made many new friends, and we developed a tight knit group. But there were groups even within our group. Many things were changing, and probably too quickly for my brain to really keep up.

The unfortunate death of my best friend Vanessa's father changed everything. She changed, and more than I realized at the time, more than I was probably able to understand. Her beautiful carefree and often a little crazy spirit turned cold and angry. She wasn't the same person; she was distant. I rarely saw her smile.

As a child I was sad for her, but I don't think I really understood. I couldn't help; I didn't know how to. Sad, grieving, people made me uncomfortable because I never knew what to do. I never had the right thing to say—is there even a *right* thing to say?

I had no experience, no script to draw from, and so I too, was lost.

Even today, looking back I feel sad for my friend, but I am sure that I do not "feel" this the way other people do. Not the way people think I *should*, and it is a source of deep internal guilt. How can I feel so disconnected, so clinical, so matter-of-fact about such events? What kind of person is like that? I must be awful.

I still carry this guilt even though I know the truth of it; the truth about autism and empathy. Autistic people *do* empathize in the strictest definition of the word. *"The intellectual identification with or vicarious experiencing of the feelings, thoughts, or attitudes of another."* I think the problem is that during our youth we have less intellect and experiences to draw from, and may appear more aloof and uncaring. That is not at all the case. We care; we feel; we hurt; but sometimes we cannot show it no matter how much we want to.

I think this may have been what happened to me back then. My heart hurts even now penning these words, thinking back to my friend, and realizing that I was probably very little comfort when she needed me most. It makes tears flood my eyes because I wish I could go back and find a way out of myself to let her know how much I truly cared about her, what she was feeling, and what she was going through.

I know that there was nothing different I was capable of at the time; I do. All I was able to do was withdraw, to pull a little further away, and spiral into the madness my own life had become.

I succumbed to that internal guilt; to that inner voice who told me that I was a terrible, uncaring, human being. Autism literature says that we lack empathy, but with more life experiences to draw from I wholly disagree.

Empathy is about identifying with other people; seeing yourself in their reflections. That is something that as a younger person I could not do. I did not see my reflection anywhere. There was no one else in my world that was like me. Only as an adult, after diagnosis, did I finally begin to see my reflection.

For the first time in my life I found others who *looked* like me. I had something contextually sound to relate to, which makes all the difference.

Empathy for autistics is about relations. The person, situation, and/or feelings, must in some way be related to us or our experiences. We must consciously direct our intellect to sift through our experiences so that we may understand what another is going through. It is extremely difficult, if not impossible, to relate to something or someone who is wholly disconnected from ourselves. Even when there is a connection, our responses may not be what is considered "normal" by others, but make sense to us.

Despite a need for a situation to relate to myself, I stand firm on the issue of empathy. I do not lack empathy; I crave it. I search it out, I look for it, and I track down books, pictures, paintings, hungrily looking, searching, needing to find a glimpse, a reflection of me.

This search is not a new occurrence; it is a search I began long ago.

Middle school and the beginning of my high school years were a glorious time of carefree oblivion. I was unenlightened, and off kilter, but assumed it was not me who was "off" but the world around me. I had been searching for something; something I could never place my finger upon. Even when I was unaware of my search, it did not go unnoticed by my friends.

They didn't understand me, or what I was looking for. The fact is, neither did I; I barely knew I was searching at all. The truth of it is, I was, I was searching for me.

Recently an old friend of mine stumbled upon my Asperger's Syndrome (AS) and writing blog. She made this comment, *"You seem to have found that thing you were always searching for and could never grasp..."* Doesn't everyone search in this manner? I'd never considered that others would not think, experience, and see life as I did. They confounded me with their thoughts and actions.

I had never shared my diagnosis with my friend, or with anyone for that matter. My own siblings have not been privy to what I had discovered about myself—to my diagnosis. I'm not hiding it, I just don't share; it doesn't come naturally.

My journey has always been a solo one, with little need to include others. The truth is it is also a journey with little thought of including others.

On the outside this looks like I am running around haphazardly jumping into situations without thinking, but that's not true. I think about situations probably more than I ought to, weigh choices, endlessly analyzing possible outcomes. The fact that I don't share my thoughts, ideas, or interests with others does not mean that I do not have them.

I have often been insulted by such accusations as, "you don't think before you do something," or "you should have talked to us about it." Why? I truly could not fathom why I would share my thoughts, or discuss my actions prior to executing them. To my mind this makes absolutely no sense. I have thought something through, came to a decision, and acted upon my decision. Isn't this the way everyone functions? Shouldn't it be?

My failure to share may have been an integral part of my immunity to peer pressure. I never asked for anyone else's input, nor did I want it most of the time. I worked out what to do on my own, without the need for others to validate my reasoning. To me, this is normal. Finding out what a group thinks before I make a decision, is not me thinking for myself.

In order to stand behind a decision I make, I must make it myself and have the confidence in that decision to act. This confidence is what defined my adolescence—my need for no one, my ability to think for myself.

Chapter Eleven: The High School Hopping Aspie

"If you liked being a teenager, there's something really wrong with you."

~ Steven King

Maybe Stephen King is right! I can admit that the high school years were an absolutely insane time. But as crazy as it was, I have some of my fondest memories in this period of my life like getting up every day, doing my hair, getting dressed, waiting for my friends to show up at my house in the morning to walk to the candy store.

I spent my first semester of high school at Franklyn Delano Roosevelt (FDR) High School in Brooklyn. The first semester was filled with ideas, homework, hopes, and dreams that quickly were pushed aside. During freshman semester one, I joined the student government, tried out for a play, the drama club, and twirling team— none of which captured my interest enough to last more than a couple of weeks.

It didn't take long to figure out that things were changing. I felt like an earthling walking in the midst of a sea of Martians. Today, I feel like I am from another planet, but back then I assumed that I was the normal one, and those people around me must have been from somewhere else. Their ideas, emotions and actions, were completely foreign. I could never figure out what made people act the way they do, and others could not figure out what made me act the way I did.

I hated FDR... that is what I told myself after just one short semester. I wanted to go to John Dewey High School to participate in their dance program. It seems that dance was the only thing that held my attention; the only thing I can pinpoint caring about. Since I had not applied to the school during my eighth grade year, and I didn't live within the school zone, I needed a special variance from the school district in order to attend. The variance was denied—no John Dewey for me.

If I couldn't go to the school I wanted, then I would go to no school at all.

During seventh grade, I briefly joined a cheerleading squad at St. Dominick's church. A friend of mine, introduced me to the squad, and to Jeannine who had cheered at St. Dominick's. Jeannine and I became friends over the next couple of years. She attended a different junior high school than I was zoned for, but when high school began, we found ourselves zoned for the same school.

Beginning in the second semester of freshman year, Jeannine walked to my house every morning before school—if she hadn't already spent the night. I had a horrible time trying to look good to go to school. Nothing was ever right, my clothes all looked "wrong," my hair was always "wrong," when all the girls around me looked beautiful in my eyes. My self-image was beginning to falter.

If we were actually heading to school, we would have been late each and every single day. But we weren't heading to school; we were heading to the candy store. Yes—we left the house each day and spend our entire school day in the candy store hanging out, went home, and repeated the same thing the next day.

Years later we often laughed at how silly our routine was; we could have just stayed in bed and slept in. I never pretended to go to school. In fact, I could have saved myself plenty of beatings from my father if I had just made up a lie that I was in school, but I didn't. When asked, I just told them that I didn't go.

If I was going to stand by my decision to not go to school then at least I would have to be truthful about that decision.

Our time was spent lollygagging the days away at Sal's Candy Store, or roaming around the campus of Kingsborough Community College. When the weather turned warmer our days were spent lying on the beach or on rolls of aluminum foil we placed on Vanessa's roof to help tan ourselves. We baked ourselves like chicken cutlets, thoroughly covering ourselves with baby oil and iodine, or cooking oil if that was all we had. There were not that many skin cancer warnings back then.

By the beginning of sophomore year, I'd had enough of the candy store. That didn't mean I was going to FDR because my mind was made up— set in stone against it. I couldn't change that decision even if I wished it. A friend from junior high, Robyn, was attending Catholic school. She went to Fontebonne Hall Academy. I could do that; I could wear a uniform.

My insistence on going to Fontebonne Hall had nothing to do with academics, and everything to do with becoming someone different—again. I could *be* one of those girls; the ones who looked cute in their Catholic school girl uniforms; the ones who belonged somewhere. I built this new image of myself up in my head, and when my parents told me they could not afford to send me to the school I had a complete meltdown.

I screamed, cried, and accused them of not caring about me, of not loving me. I threw things in a fit of rage that I still fail to grasp. This was the first time I can recall have a rage meltdown, which was followed by two days of sleeping. This must have scared the wits out of my parents because when the two days of sleep had passed they announced that I could attend Fontebonne.

The first day of school, for me was in October of my sophomore year of high school. Even though I didn't attend many classes at FDR, I still managed to pop into the rooms enough to pass the exams. Attendance was an issue. My test scores were high enough to fight for me to pass the class even though I only attended on test days. I was a very good test taker.

I remember dressing in my brand new uniform, complete with tights, school sweater and black shoes. I don't know exactly what I expected from this new life of mine. Did I think that everything would be different, people would be different, school would be different, just because I put on a plaid skirt? Apparently, I did, and was soon gravely disappointed. Instead of being a part of this group, a part of this new school community, I was more of an outcast than ever.

The girls that attended that school were nothing like me. I suppose no one was.

My time in Catholic school did not last very long. The first time my mother had to come up to school was to discuss my tardiness. It was nearly impossible for me to arrive to school on time. It didn't matter what time I left the house, if it was late, or early, I managed to show up at school late.

It wasn't intentional; stuff just always happened to me. If I wasn't falling on my way to the bus stop and tearing my stockings, I was leaving my books home needing to go back. More than once the bus pulled to the curb sending a wave of muddy water from the previous rainfall into my face and hair.

Days that I managed to make it to the bus stop, *and onto the bus,* without incident often ended in my wandering the streets of Bay Ridge wondering *why I had turned up this block.* No matter how many times I exited the bus on Fourth Avenue, and started to the walk up to the school, I managed to find myself lost in the streets. The minute I hit the avenues that were not numbered the way I'd been used to I felt lost.

Maybe I was just lost in my own world again, and failed to pay attention to the street signs, or maybe I was struggling with what I now know is called place-blindness. Eventually I found my route, and as long as I continued on the same route, traveling the exact same streets each time, I would not be lost.

Having my route sorted allowed me to arrive at school on time some of the days, which was a definite improvement, but by that time I was already labeled. I was expected to be late, to be trouble, to not follow the rules—intentionally. The walls were closing in around me and I began longing to be free of that place.

Rules without logic were ones that I was incapable of following. It was test day, and a fever was not keeping me away from test day. Doing well on tests was the only thing that redeemed my school life. The day I showed up to take my Biology Regents exam was my last day at Fontebonne Hall Academy.

There was this one nun who hated me. I had her for my first period class, and since I was never on time I was the problem child. I can't tell you how happy I was to not have her proctoring the test.

School rules: Students are not allowed to wear jackets in class. All students must be dressed in proper school uniforms.

The problem was that I was burning up with fever, and freezing. The lousy thin navy blue V-necked school sweater was not keeping me warm enough. Explaining this to the proctor, she allowed me to wear my coat during the test.

My teeth were chattering while I filled in the tiny circles on the answer sheet that would be scanned into the computer system. My head ached, and my nose was running, but I was almost done then I would go home sick.

I didn't see her enter the room.

"Wearing coats are not permitted in class," a squeaky voice screamed. The pencil flew out of my hands and broke on the floor when she snatched my arm to pull me out of my seat. "Get that coat off!"

My first period teacher stood in front of me. What was she doing here? The nun proctoring the test began to rise from her seat when the crazy woman glared at her. "I'll handle this," she said," Let's go young lady."

When tugging on my arm didn't have the desired effect, she grabbed a fist full of my hair to pull me from the desk.

"Don't touch me!" I screamed, and before I knew it she had a fist full of my hair, and I had a fist full of hers. That is exactly how we proceeded to the office, both of us refusing to let go of the other's locks.

I was "not Fontebonne material", that's what my mother was told that afternoon when they sent me on my way home.

"Now what are you going to do?" my mother said.

"Cathy, that nun should not have touched her," my grandmother said, but my mother didn't seem to hear her.

I sat at my kitchen table while my mother yelled. My father was happy not to have to pay the tuition bill any longer but said little else. Why was no one else upset that that woman pulled my hair? Why was I the one who was wrong just because I pulled her hair back? That makes no sense! Why were the rules different just because she was an adult? Shouldn't she have been made to act more appropriately?

I was never given an opportunity to explain why I was wearing my coat in the first place, no one asked, no one cared.

We had already established I would not attend FDR; that decision was final, and I was immovable. The law required that I attend high school or I would have been just as satisfied with not going to school at all. I could not even enroll in "mini-school".

Mini-School was a half day GED program that required I be past my sixteenth birthday, which was still a few months away.

My mother tried to force me to re-enroll at FDR but I told them plainly that if they made me attend that school I would not show up.

"We will send the police to your house, and they will force you to come to school," a woman in charge of admissions said.

"Someone needs to blow-up this school. This school sucks!" I yelled, and swiped my arm across the papers hanging off the front of her desk sending them sailing through the air before storming out.

I didn't say I *would* blow up the school, or even that I wanted to blow up the school. I was just so angry that I felt like I would punch a hole through the wall. Everything was being blamed on me, it was always all my fault and I was helpless to do anything about it.

Apparently, you cannot just say anything you want without consequences. You are not allowed to say blow-up and school in the same sentence. Now—I was not allowed to return to FDR, even if I wanted to, which was fine with me!

I was called down to the superintendent's office for district 20 schools, and *questioned* about what I intended to do to the school. I did not intend to do anything.

"Would you consider sending her to an alternative high school?" he asked my mother. But it really was not a question at all, I had no choice in the matter, neither did my mother. I had to comply, do as he said, or *pay the price*, his words. When I asked him exactly what the price would be, he glared at me.

I really wanted to know; maybe the price I'd have to pay would be worth it.

"Brooklyn College Academy (BCA), that is where we are going to send her," he said to my mother without taking his eyes off of me. "They can keep a good eye on her." *Could they now?*

I liked BCA. It is an alternative high school that is on the campus of Brooklyn College. Even some of the college staff was unaware of its presence. This school was as optional as a school could get. If I wanted to sit in the hallways of the college instead of attending class, that was fine. If I wanted to roam the campus endlessly, that was all right too. As long as I signed in when school began, the rest of the day was mine, until it was time to sign out.

I spent those days sitting in the hall reading books, and wandering the campus in my own world. No one really cared what I did during the day; they were only required to *keep us kids out of trouble*. I don't know how exactly they were accomplishing that directive if they had no idea where we were or how we spent our days.

My sixteenth birthday was approaching quickly, and I was preoccupied with my upcoming Sweet Sixteen party. Putting school pretty far out of my mind because once I turned sixteen no one could force me to go to school any longer. Even mini-school was out of the question since it met at FDR, and I, for all intents and purposes was completely banned from stepping foot on that campus. Without the mini-school program, I could wait until I was seventeen and take the GED test on my own. Who needs school anyway?

In July of 1991, after my seventeenth birthday I promptly signed up to take the GED exam. The test took eight hours covering all the subjects that I supposedly should have covered in H.S. You know—the high school that I didn't attend.

I passed that test on the first try just a couple points shy of the highest score possible. For kicks I took the SAT test to see how I would do, and scored in the 1400 range. I was told that was an excellent score. Deciding to leave high school behind, and be someone, or someone else, I enrolled in John Jay College of Criminal Justice in the fall of 1991, one full year before my peers were to graduate high school. Academics came easily to me. The rest of life— not so much.

Chapter Twelve: Autism Widens the Divide; Life Outside My Bubble

The divide was widening; the divide that separated me from the rest of the world. In the years leading up to high school I hadn't noticed it. I didn't feel it. I was fairly oblivious. I trudged through life in my own world bouncing around in my bubble.

I didn't notice how different I felt from the people around me, or how truly different my thoughts and ideas were. But as I traveled through my early teens I began to feel it. The gap was broad and wide, and growing deeper with each passing year.

Each section of my life is fairly compartmentalized in my brain. I remember having friends for a time period and when the time was left behind so were the friends. I had difficulty incorporating more than one person into my life at a time, making it very difficult to juggle the complications of relationships that were to come.

Even when it came to my closest friends, I had trouble incorporating both of them. My two friends drew closer to each other, and I drifted further away. It was not intentional, they didn't exclude me—to an extent I excluded myself. When I didn't understand the dynamics, couldn't relate to the situation, or flat-out disagreed with their actions I withdrew, removed myself, and disappeared.

Relationships became more complicated, and that was a difficult thing for me to navigate. My inability to have more than one friend at a time made it difficult for me to relate to others, and keep friends when I developed other relationships—romantic relationships.

Often times if I had a boyfriend as a teenager, my friends rarely saw me. It was, again, all or nothing. I was with that one person to the exclusion of everyone and usually everything else. I didn't understand their need for time away, or their need for time with their own friends because I had no such needs.

Throughout high school I was known for vanishing when a boy I liked came around. I gave no thought whatsoever to just leaving with him without telling my friends I was going. It never crossed my mind most of the time. I switched from friend mode to girlfriend mode. I couldn't stay in two modes at the same time.

I never thought anyone would wonder where I was, after all, I knew where I was. Didn't they? An outsider looking in with a keenly trained eye may have noticed my mind-blindness when I was a child, but I would not have.

Looking back with a new set of eyes, armed with the knowledge of my autism, I can clearly see just how much I *didn't see*— *I didn't see past me.* It wasn't an intentional self-absorption; I hadn't even realized I was doing it.

Inside the gaping divide between what others perceive and what my brain processed was a dangerous place. This danger was greatest at a time when I was most vulnerable, at a time when I was developing my sense of self, my elusive identity, my self-image.

I learned to socialize by emulation. Unfortunately, I learned about body image and what a "real woman" looks like in magazines—Penthouse magazines. This caused mind-blinding damage to my self-image.

I remember the first time I found my father's stash of magazines, kept tucked in his nightstand drawer. They weren't exactly hidden since I could open the drawer at will and peer inside. You would think I'd be appalled but I wasn't. I was fascinated, intrigued.

Flipping through the pages, I viewed each beautiful woman with their perfect smiles, perfect hair, tanned skin, and smooth curves. One day, I would look like that—and one day I did.

I am thankful that back then the magazines were not as explicitly graphic as they are today; however, they were graphic enough to damage my frail self-image. They set the standard for body-image unrealistically high, and the reward for achieving this image low and degrading.

My short time wearing a Catholic school uniform taught me one thing—short skirts attracted attention. The magazines reinforced this attention getting strategy. And it wasn't just adult magazines, teen magazines, fashion magazines, they all told young girls the same thing—you must look like *this*, whatever this was at the time.

Shirts became shorter, pants tighter, tops cut lower—attracting more attention than any teenage girl should receive, let alone one whose danger radar doesn't not function properly. Beyond the obvious dangers that attracting too much attention from the opposite sex, and older ones at that, a much bigger unforeseen danger lurked—*mind blindness.*

One of the first things that I learned about my Asperger's diagnosis is that there are three core deficits that accompany this condition—the lack of theory of mind, executive dysfunction, and weak central coherence. There are also a host of other issues like sensory processing difficulties—being hyper or hypo sensitive to outside stimuli like to heat, cold, or pain.

Theory of Mind is the ability to understand that other people's feelings, intentions, and desires are different than your own, and then interpret, infer, or predict their actions. It is a fundamental understanding that their actions are based on their inner feelings. Autistic people often lack, or have great difficulty with theory of mind—they are said to be mind-blind.

Being mind-blind makes you extremely susceptible to deception. The mind-blind, autistic teenaged girl may not see the signs that are obvious to everyone else around them. They do not pick up on social cues, vocal intonations, or facial expression. Or, if they noticed they often will misinterpret their meanings. Picking up on social cues comes naturally to the neurotypical (NT) individual, a person who is not autistic, but for those with autism this innate ability is missing.

Missing social cues can be awkward in social situations leaving you doing or saying the wrong thing at the wrong times. It may cause the autistic person to run over other people when they are talking, not waiting for them to finish. They do not pick up the cue that it is their turn to speak. There is often also no filter between brain and mouth. Whatever pops into the brain usually flies out of the mouth making the autistic person extremely blunt, sometimes appearing rude.

There can be many consequences of missing social clues, but none may be more devastating, dangerous, and harmful than not seeing the signs within your own relationships, particularly ones with the opposite sex.

Chapter Thirteen: The Dangers of the Teenaged Autistic Girl and Her First Loves: Mind-Blindness

First loves, obsessions, passions, special interests, call it whatever you want, they can captivate and completely blind any young teenage girl's mind. Girls are swept away in the idea of first love, the knight in shining armor, and forever after. This is a glorious time of love, learning to love, loss and pain; the time that mothers worry about their daughters, and fathers buy shot-guns.

Some girls caught up in the sweeping whirlwind of first love do not see the signs of the impending crash at the end of the road. They love idealistically, but after the hurt and broken bones heal they learn to take another look to watch for the road signs. Autistic girls not only do not see the signs, but they don't see them the next time they are headed into the same brick wall either.

It happened over and over again, I missed the signs. I didn't see them coming. I was left blindsided, alone and confused. I didn't see the warnings; I didn't see the road posts; I barreled down love's highway at top speed with no breaks—every time.

I don't get "hints", I need direct language. Subtleties are lost on me. If you are not completely direct, and *tell me something is wrong* with the relationship, I will assume all is well. If all is well with me, then all is well with you. If it were not, you would have directly said something, wouldn't you? If something I did bothered you, or I did something wrong, you wouldn't pretend everything was fine, would you? I wouldn't.

I always assumed that I understood people. I prided myself in being honest, upfront, and direct, assuming that everyone else around me behaved in the same manner. If you were in my life that meant I trusted you, and if I trusted you, I believed you. It was as simple as that.

I was just fourteen and attracted the attention of a boy older than I was. Smart, handsome, cool, and he could dance, what more did I need? The problem was he had a girlfriend; at least, it should have been a problem. Since his girlfriend was eighteen, and I was only fourteen, I was honored that he would come to my house when she was at work and that he hung out with me during my days at the candy store. After all, he was just trying to figure out a way to break up with her gently—for six months.

I began to obsess about him, seeing him whenever I could even if just for a few minutes sitting on my front porch in the night. It may have continued on forever, me waiting and believing, if someone else didn't walk into my life and wipe him off the map. That is the way it worked with me. I didn't hide it, "Sorry, I met someone else; now, go away."

I never thought to be deceitful or even gentle for that matter. I told the truth very matter-of-factly. If I moved on from one interest to another they must have also and I put them out of my mind.

According to the DSM-IV(Diagnostic and Statistical Manual of Mental Disorders), the diagnostic criteria for Asperger's Syndrome (AS), having an *"encompassing preoccupation with one or more stereotyped and restricted patterns of interest that is abnormal either in intensity or focus"* is a core symptom of AS.

I've had many special interests, preoccupations, passions, obsessions through the years beginning as young as three years old. My three year old self was completely preoccupied with baseball; my fifteen year old self—boys, or more precisely a boy.

That is not an unusual preoccupation for a fifteen year old girl, but what we need to look at is the intensity and focus. When focused on an interest to the exclusion of everything else, and everyone else in your life, is this not considered obsession? For the autistic person our obsessions and passions are soothing, calming, a place to hide, decompress, regenerate—a place of quiet peace. But what happens when your special interest, your obsession, is a person?

Love can be joyous and healthy but obsession can be seen as unwanted attention, smothering affection, and in the extreme…stalking. To make matters worse, the mind-blind teenager will usually never know if she steps over this line. How much is too much exactly?

The first few months were perfect. We cruised the neighborhood with the windows down, wind in my hair—and his, which was possibly longer than my own. My friends faded into the background of my mind, nothing else mattered, no one else existed. I was in my "one friend, one person allowed in my life at a time," mode—other people were far from my thoughts.

I went to school—ok, to the candy store, went to McDonald's, where I was working as a cashier, work, and then hopped into his car at night to drive around. I wanted to stay roaming the neighborhoods like that all night long, but he needed to meet his friends. Every night around eleven o'clock he dropped me off at home and left to hang out with the guys.

At first I tried to be accommodating, to make him happy. I needed to be home before midnight or my father would flip out anyway, I told myself. But as time went on it became harder, and harder to let go—to understand this strange need for his friends. Why not just stay hanging out with me? What was wrong with me? I began to take it personally, not understanding that others may have feelings and needs different than my own. I couldn't see it; I couldn't understand it; his behavior made no sense to me.

"If you loved me, you'd stay!"

On New Year's Eve we had a fight. He didn't stay. I called and left messages on his voicemail like a crazy stalker, hung-up and redialed again. The return calls never came. What did I do wrong?

For the next few months I could think of nothing else. He wouldn't even speak to me, giving no reason at all.

I began dating someone else, just to keep my mind off things and keep myself occupied. Make no mistake about it; he knew all about my obsession with my ex-boyfriend, and how I desperately wanted him to dance with me at my sweet sixteen. Why that boy hung around me I'll never know.

It had never occurred to me that I was hurting someone's feelings, how could I if I was truthful with them? He knew that if my ex showed up at my Sweet Sixteen party, that it would be the end of things. I told him I would let him dance with me on my birthday *if* you-know-who didn't show up. I was still holding out hope. I'd invited him, and I thought maybe just maybe he would show-up and surprise me—and he did.

The night was a blur; we were back together and that is how it would always be, wouldn't it? I'd never considered any other scenario in my head—ever.

These relationships were all encompassing; I wanted to spend every free moment together and assumed that he wanted that too.

Life at home with my parents was getting more difficult. I fought with my father constantly. He was violent when he drank, and I was antagonistic. I truly didn't care what he thought, what he said, or what he did. I had no respect for him whatsoever. My father demanding my blind obedience and respect was a ridiculous notion in my mind. "Respect needs to be earned," I told him. My father's response was always the same, "I'm your father, and you had better respect me."

That never worked. I couldn't pretend, I told him the truth, and it got me beat—again. It was during that time I really noticed my hypo-sensitivity to pain. If I withdrew into myself, and put on a calm face, I felt no pain. He could throw me, punch me, fling me down the stairs, and I was able to stand and say, "Go ahead, do it again. Why don't you just kill me this time?"

I had two responses to my father's violence; a withdrawal and calm or a violent fighting back. This night, after the violent explosion, he threw me out and told me not to come back, so I left.

I only allowed the tears to flow when I got to the train station up the block. My hands trembled as I dialed my boyfriend's home phone number and sobbed into the receiver. His sister answered the phone. After hearing my sobs she hopped in her car and picked me up. I spent the next couple of months sleeping on their sofa.

I tried to join a new family. It made no real difference to me that this family was not my own. They took me in, included me, and cared for me. It also didn't matter what my boyfriend at the time thought about the situation. He never talked to me about it, I guess I was supposed to see the signs; get the "hints", but I didn't.

It only took him a couple of weeks to mysteriously stop speaking to me again. This was the second time he had done this—just cut me out without an explanation or without talking to me. I thought we would talk tomorrow, in fact, every day I thought we would talk tomorrow. Months went by and tomorrow never came. I never once considered that he simply didn't want me there. When the family was preparing to move, I assumed I was going with them. His mom had a new daughter now—me.

I didn't understand the subtleties, only a direct approach worked and I was stunned. When his mom had to break it to me after weeks of hinting I was devastated. She couldn't allow me to live with them if her son didn't want me there. She was right of course, but how did I not see this coming? Was I so inside of my own world, in my own head, that I was constantly misinterpreting the people around me?

"AS makes it difficult to learn from where you have been. It makes it difficult to generalize and problem solve." ~ Liane Holliday Willey. Pretending to be Normal: Living with Asperger's Syndrome

I did not learn from this situation, I did not see the signs the next time around. This was twice the same person shut me out without speaking to me, and I never considered it would happen again, but of course, it did.

About a year later, when I was beginning college, we were back together again, and I was back to my old self—misinterpreting, misunderstanding, and assuming his intentions were the same as my own. Together forever, every waking moment, sharing life and every breath—an adolescent idealistic look at life and love, one I should have long since shed.

I didn't change; he didn't change, and I am sure by now I don't have to tell you how that episode ended, because if you guessed that it ended much in the same manner as the last two times you would be correct. How could I be so stupid? So blind?

He flew off to Daytona Beach for Spring Break with his friends. Assuming he would be thrilled to see me, I surprised him, I showed up. I drove 800 miles to be with him, to affect my surprise, and he pushed me away. He needed to be with his friends. In the end he ignored me and would not speak to me at all.

Chapter Fourteen: The Autistic College Student: Conjured Confidence, Failed Relationships, and Executive Dysfunction

I had no sense of self, in many ways I still struggle with this today. Constantly having difficulty knowing who I am, or how I want to be is disorienting. I jumped from persona to persona, from emulation to emulation, until I found something that worked.

My self-image was in shambles, a mess of which I had no idea how to clean up. I couldn't understand what was wrong with me, or why people pushed me away. Why was I never enough? Why did others want more than just me? I didn't need more than just them. In fact, I couldn't incorporate more than just them.

The social scenes surrounding my late teens and early twenties were focused in bars and nightclubs. This environment would have been the cause of near immediate sensory overload had it not been for the alcohol. I made a habit of chugging down as many drinks as possible within the first few minutes of an outing. This way I was free from the head pounding music, and all the voices talking at the same time.

I was able to dance in my own world on the dance floor for hours on end, until I either couldn't stand or couldn't hold one more ounce of liquor. I didn't need to be out with friends; I could even go out alone and *make friends*. The kind I didn't need to ask their names, or bother to get to know in the morning.

My poor self-esteem was masked by a conjured self-confidence, and proven by the attention of men. I was often said to be, "just like a guy" by many of my friends. Modesty did not live in me.

I didn't understand women. Females hovered in groups giggling, and wondering if they were getting a man's attention. I never wondered, no need to, I was direct. I saw no sense in playing games, and wondering if a guy liked me.

This partying night owl I played was confident. She didn't play games. If she saw something she liked, she went after it. Rejection had no effect whatsoever on her, she simply moved on to the next guy she picked out.

I simply had no human connections. I couldn't be used for sex, because I would have been considered the user. I had no real interest in these men, just for what I'd purposed them for at the time. I couldn't be hurt because I was wholly disconnected. Connections are confusing; connections hurt.

Dancing and puberty had been good for my body image. I rivaled some of those images in the magazines. I had no need to be bashful. As a female, however, I was socially unacceptable—only men behaved in such crude ways.

The idea of these separate gender roles, these double standards baffled me. Why were things socially acceptable for men, but not for women? Who made up these rules anyway?

I spent most of my college nights on dance floors across NYC with whichever guy I fancied at the time. I was uninhibited, and popular, but not someone you would take seriously. I never took any of them seriously and fiercely pushed away any man that would try to keep any part of me for himself. I was my own person, belonged to no one, and would commit to no one. The minute someone became serious, I'd flee.

Although I worked at breaking free of anyone who would attempt to hold on to me, I eventually found myself in "love" again. I should have known better, but this one guy fought harder than the rest—he persisted even through my unspeakable cruelty.

We only knew each other for a couple of weeks before we flew off for a week's vacation in Jamaica pretending to be newlyweds. The shine of this knight's armor blinded my eyes, and the lure of "happily ever after" opened the gates that I should have slammed shut. Those walls were there for protection after all, I just didn't realize the person I needed protection from was me.

The two of us lived in a small apartment in Bay Ridge. We lived like a newly married couple, though we were not, it was a game of house. I suppose I was interesting and exciting at first, but when I let someone in, the one person was supposed to be the *only* person.

I was adopted into his group of friends, who treated me like I belonged. There was no time spent apart if we were not at work. We bowled on teams together, went out with friends together, to family outings together—lived together. So, how could I have missed it?

"I'm moving back home," he said one day out of the blue.

"What? What do you mean?"

"I'd been thinking about it for a while. I told my mother last night."

A while? We'd only lived together for three short months. He still wanted to be with me, he just did not want to live together. I, once again, was dumbfounded. I couldn't wrap my mind around what I was being told. There were no signs, no evidence of issues in our relationship, and he sure never *said* anything to me. But none of that mattered; he left me alone in that apartment with rent due and nowhere to go.

Getting what I wanted (people) came easy to me; keeping them was impossible.

If only I had someone who understood, someone who recognized the difficulties I was having maybe I would have learned to read the signs. The problem with being caught off-guard constantly was that I felt ripped out of my own life. In an instant everything changed with no warning. There was no time to adjust to a failing relationship, to resign myself to the way things were about to change, or to even try and work things out. I had no warning—ever. By the time I found out things had gone wrong, it was way past the point of fixing it. Life was chipping away at my self-esteem, my self-worth, my self-image one relationship at a time.

My first semester at John Jay College of Criminal Justice went as smoothly as I could expect. I had no problems with the academics and had straight A's across the board—easy peasy. But what I did not have was any college friends. For the most part I didn't mind, I was living back at home, and I worked two jobs. Life was busy, and that hid the fact that I was alone.

A full course load at John Jay only took up two weekdays. The remaining three I spent working as a bank teller. On the weekends I worked at a catering hall as a cocktail waitress. I was determined to not have to live back home for very long.

I had trouble staying focused and interested. I majored in Forensic Science, but chemistry didn't hold my interest. So I transferred to St. John's University in Staten Island where I took several English and Creative Writing and Psychology classes.

Girls all around me were pledging for sororities. They walked in groups, ate lunch together, and basically kept away from me. I only attracted the attention of boys, this act I already had down pat. Despite the attention I focused on my studies, St. John's only outlasted John Jay by one semester.

St. John's was also a bigger challenge than John Jay. Not because of the academics, because I found the coursework to be more difficult at John Jay; but because the campus was larger. I had a recurrence of my first experience with junior high school and place-blindness. The additional stress from constantly being lost and late for class contributed to my dropping out of college after a total of three semesters. My brain was perpetually overloaded.

Although I managed to keep straight A's during these semesters, it took so much work on my part that I was completely and utterly burned out. The course load and my growing responsibilities overcame me. I could not keep two thoughts in a row together in my mind.

Part of what made college so exhausting was my proneness to get lost in the details. One detail of a lesson, lecture, assignment, or test question would grab my focus and I would lose sight of the whole picture. If one word was wrong in a sentence or oddly placed, I was so consumed by that one small detail that I completely lost sight of what the text said, making me have to go back and re-read the entire thing.

I suspect that my autism bubbled up to the surface highlighting many of the core deficits that those with Asperger's Syndrome (AS), Autism Spectrum Disorders (ASD), and High-Functioning Autism (HFA) share. I clearly had severe deficits with theory of mind, but college life made my weak central coherence and executive dysfunction noticeable.

Central coherence is the ability to focus on both details as well as wholes. People with autism appear to have a heightened focus on details rather than wholes, a cognitive style termed 'weak central coherence'. Compounding the problem was my inability to complete tasks, stick with a plan, and work towards a long term goal. I struggled with the sequencing needed to complete the more complex tasks that working your way through college required—an example of executive dysfunction.

Executive function pertains to the way in which people monitor and control their thoughts and actions, which includes processes like working memory, planning, cognitive flexibility, and inhibitory control. Executive function is responsible for your skills and ability to goal, plan, sequence, prioritize, organize, initiate, inhibit, pace, shift, self-monitor, emotional control, and completing.

When a person with autism is experiencing executive dysfunction, they experience impairment or deficits in the higher-order processes that enable them to plan, sequence, initiate, and sustain their behaviors towards some goal, incorporating feedback and making adjustments along the way. My constant failure to complete was evident in everything I tried to accomplish. It spilled over from my school life, to my personal life, and right into my adult working life.

I had tremendous difficulty trying to figure out what was wrong with me, why I could never seem to finish anything I started. Shifting activities was a challenge, and I was terrible at pacing myself. I had two speeds—full speed ahead, and stop; there was never anything in between—all or nothing.

My father thought my going to college was stupid; that I was wasting my time and his money only to learn nonsense. He said all I needed was *street smarts,* of which I had none, and college was not going to teach me that. Maybe he saw the dysfunction that I did not, or maybe he saw something that he could not describe. But maybe he could have described me as something other than—stupid.

Going to college was stupid; I was stupid; all my ideas, thoughts, and dreams were stupid, and something to be mocked, something to be laughed at—a joke. A joke that I did not think was funny.

Financial aid didn't cover the additional tuition expenses that transferring to St. John's University brought, so in addition to my aid, and loans, I needed my father to sign for a parent's loan. He did for the first semester, whining and complaining about how it was a waste of time. But after that he refused and if I wanted to continue the finances were my problem.

He never repaid that parent loan, and a few years later the IRS confiscated his income tax refund to repay the debt. Would you believe my mother brought it up again—21 years later? Remarking how I wasted money on something I never finished.

Being a college drop-out, I was thrust into the adult working world. Surely, with my intelligence and bubbly smile I would be successful there.

Chapter Fifteen: Asperger's and the Transition to Working Chaos

I wish I could say I found my niche; I found the place where I belonged; I found the place where I could be me, be productive, and be *somebody*. But the truth is, navigating the world of working adults proved more difficult than I could have ever imagined.

I've worked as a bank teller, cashier, waitress, bartender, lab assistant, undercover investigator, emergency medical technician, secretary, dance instructor, medical transcriptionist, correctional officer, and a writer. I have some experience in marketing, web design, graphics, bookkeeping, accounting, and tax preparation. I've started, and failed at, more businesses than most people will ever try in their lifetime, but I've mastered and finished nothing.

Young, energetic and ambitious should have accounted for something, but it seemed like being at work sapped my energy. My friends and co-workers had the ability to work all day, and play through the night. They still managed to get up and get to work on time the next day. I had difficulty opening my eyes the next morning.

By the time I made it home from a day of work, a day of interacting with the world around me, I was exhausted.

I don't mean to say I was tired; we all get tired. I was utterly, drop on the floor, and cannot peel my eyelids open tired. Staying in touch with friends, making phone calls, and socializing was not even a thought in my mind. I barely managed to work a full day, go home sleep, and get up the next morning. Being able to hyper-focus on a task, and learn very quickly, I was able to learn anything I needed to, anything I wanted to, making me very good at any job I took. At least I was good at it for a while—a very short while.

Within a few short weeks of beginning a job I was unable to maintain an appropriate schedule and arrived to work late on most days. As stress levels rose I became completely incapable of keeping two thoughts together in my head in a row, and usually wound up with a series of strange ailments. Panic and oftentimes dread began to emerge when mornings were approaching because I knew I needed to be up and at work in a few hours. My lifelong insomnia never allowed me to get more than a couple of hours of sleep in a row. As dawn approached the stress built; I should have been sleeping.

By the time I fell asleep it was almost time to wake, and then I couldn't get out of bed. The days that I was up on time, I could not find my keys, my shoes, my purse, or my metro card. Even on the days that I would have been on time, something happened to put me running behind.

I was falling way behind in life while the rest of the world zoomed past me at a blinding speed, effortlessly, leaving me in the dust to choke on my own failures and guilt.

Being young without many responsibilities made it easy for me to hop from job to job much to the annoyance of those around me. For the most part, I didn't mind because I was moving on, trying something new, starting over again. I began to gravitate to night jobs—bartending and waitressing. These jobs brought in the most money for me at the time, and negated the need to sleep at night and rise in the morning. Arriving on time at 8 p.m. was infinitely easier than 8 a.m., and more in tune with my insomnia.

Even the night jobs, however, did not last long. Those particular professions require incredible people skills, memory and dexterity. Bombarded by people requiring my social interaction interfered with my ability to perform basic tasks.

Bars are loud. Music blasts in the background, while dozens of people are calling for your attention at the same time hollering drink orders at you. You are expected to not only make the drinks, but remember who gets which drink.

My elbow hit the glasses. Everyone recognized the crash. I often was embarrassed by applause in the diner when that happened. The spilled drinks caused me to slip on my way to get a mop. There was no applause; laughter and cursing—yes, but at least there was no clapping.

Flustered, I tried to regain my composure and distribute the remainder of my orders. No one received the right drink on the first try. I could not remember who ordered what. I often had all the drinks done correctly but upon turning to face the customers it was like looking at group of strangers—ones that I did not just speak with two minutes earlier. By the time the drink confusion was sorted out, I didn't remember who I collected money from, or whose change was in my hand.

Suspecting I was giving away free drinks, I was let go—another job bites the dust. I was not giving away free drinks—I don't think—well, at least not on purpose. I suspect that my fumbling did probably cause customers to take advantage of me and walk away with their drinks without paying. I truly had no way of knowing, which made me an easy mark.

I never questioned a customer who said they paid because I assumed that they were telling the truth. The idea that I was being lied to, or taken advantage of never crossed my mind. The owner didn't understand how I could be so stupid. Either that or I was letting customers get away with their drinks intentionally.

My brain was atrophying; I could feel it. I wanted to do more with my life. I was too smart to spend all my time serving drinks. Realizing that there was no way I could go back to college, knowing already that I did not have the capacity to follow through and stick with something as long-term as a four-year college degree, I decided to become an Emergency Medical Technician (EMT).

The basic EMT course only lasts a couple of months, which was about my limit in terms of attention and dedication. I knew I could make it through a few months of training so I enrolled in the Training Institute for Medical Emergencies and Rescue. The course began in February, concluding with a state examination in June.

I love information, facts, knowledge. Class work was easy; I had absolutely no issues with academics. In fact, medical terminology felt like a natural second language, a language I learned quickly. I had difficulty with the practical exams and applications of emergency medical procedures but my academic scores boosted my self-confidence so I pressed forward. After completing the coursework, and passing the practical applications examinations, I sat for the state exam.

A couple of weeks later my test results were mailed to my home—97 out of 100! I should have been thrilled but I was disturbed. Three points—where did I lose three points? What questions did I answer incorrectly? Could those questions, my mistakes, my lack of knowledge in that area cost someone their life? This was no laughing matter. There was no cause to celebrate. What if I was in the field and made a critical mistake?

Those three points crippled my self-confidence, and made me question every decision I needed to make. Could this decision be the one thing I got wrong on the test?

Despite my rattled confidence, I truly wanted to do something worthwhile, to help people. It had not occurred to me that my five foot nothing stature would hinder my ability to get a paying job in the field. Or that the fact I weighed just over a hundred pounds soaking wet would cause employers to higher less intelligent, but larger men to hoist patients on stretchers in and out of homes. Unfortunately, this was a part of the job I had not considered. Who wants a small female who could not lift patients up and down the stairs of a five-story walk up in NYC as a partner?

I was dejected. I finally finished something. I completed the course, I received my state certification, but for what?

My need to do something important, to help people, and to make a difference in the world, led me to apply to work for a volunteer ambulance service. I loved it! I volunteered for overnight shifts, where we slept on cots until the sirens rang when a call came in. They had no problem allowing me to volunteer and placing me as the "third-man" on the crew. Two men were still needed to carry patients, but there was still plenty to do that didn't' involve lifting.

I had the often unique ability to stay calm in emergency situations, to remain un-rattled by the tragedy around me, and to drown people out because I had a job to do. I could put human interaction way in the back of my mind and focus on the task at hand.

What I thought was my strength—my calm face, was actually looked upon as something quite different—uncaring, unfeeling. My being seen as uncaring, without feelings for those around me, could not have been further from the truth. I was out there *volunteering* on an ambulance precisely because I do care. I loved being out there— helping, making a difference.

Shortly after I became an EMT, there was an accident in front of my house. I saw it; the old man flew through the air. He must not have been watching where he was going. He stepped out from between two parked cars into four lanes of traffic on 65th street just off of the corner. He landed on 19th Avenue about thirty feet from where he started.

There was no thought, just training, and protocol. Being only a half of a block away, I reached him just before he was gone—but only just. There was nothing I could do, but I knew protocol. I began CPR immediately, instructed bystanders to call 911, and continued compressions until help arrived.

The Fire Department was the first on the scene, as was usual being that they were only a couple of blocks away. Unfortunately they were used to responding to our street. I grew up watching too many people die on that corner. It was a terrible place for traffic accidents. One side of our block had a huge hill—from 63-64th streets, from that side of the hill you were able to see the traffic light on 65th street. All too often drivers seeing a green light about to turn yellow, or red, would come flying over that hill and try to race through the light on the next block, darting across four lanes of traffic. Too often, they didn't make it; something or someone got in their way.

After the ambulance arrived, the paramedics took over chest compressions which I had continued while the firemen ventilated the man lying in the street. They slipped a back board under him, lifted him onto a stretcher, and into the ambulance. He was already gone, we all knew it, but it was not our job to make that determination. Our job was to provide cardio-pulmonary resuscitation until a doctor at the hospital takes over, or instructs us to stop.

The ambulance roared down the street; I watched it go before turning to head inside. I had forgotten that my boyfriend at the time was even standing there. I was focused on my task. Inside I washed all the blood from my hands and arms. I hadn't realized until then how much blood there had been. Then I headed to my room to "hang-out" as if nothing had happened.

I didn't understand what the fuss was all about. When my father returned home from work he was worried about me. He thought I was locked up in my room distraught. He was concerned that a man had died, quite literally in my hands, and thought I would or should have been a mess. I looked at him like he had two heads, and that concerned him more than anything.

I was not cold, or uncaring. I had feelings—many of them. My father thought I would blame myself and be a wreck because I couldn't save him. I desperately wanted to save him; that is why I ran to help, but in this instance I didn't blame myself. It was cut and dry, it was not my fault, and I could only do my part. I was a trained professional.

I still remember the beautiful letters the old man's widow and son wrote to me. They lived around the corner from our house; the man had stepped out into the street right in front of his home. The letters thanked me for trying to help him. The letters saddened me. I felt saddened by that family's loss, but I did not feel what others thought I should, or react in the way they thought I should have.

Despite constantly being filled with a confusing and often contradicting array of emotions, my own internal turmoil, I was emotionally detached from other people—emotionally detached from most of the world around me. In certain situations that emotional detachment proved to be a gift.

I was a rigidly inconsistent worker. Of all the issues I can list, and the list is long, the single most destructive behavior to my early working life was my inability to be consistent-particularly my inability to be on-time. I have lost countless jobs for no other reason than I simply could not stay on someone else's schedule. The more demanding the job, the people I needed to deal with, or the more sensory stimuli involved, the quicker my downward spiral of inconsistency began.

I'm a sprinter, not a marathon runner—of this much I am certain. I need to engage in activities where I take off running and get across the finish line fairly quickly. I have no stamina in the sense that long term goals, planning, and projects never come to fruition. They somehow get lost along the way, either pushed to the side by my countless detours, or I am left behind, lost in the rear view mirror while I examine the imperfection of the painted yellow lines in the road.

I could spend days at work being extraordinarily productive, weeks in fact, but those are one of my little inconsistencies. Productivity was generally followed closely by days of meandering through life getting lost in the tiniest of details. I didn't waste my days away intentionally—time just meant very little, or should I say I had no perception of time. The days got away from me, hours passed, and I barely noticed.

Time has never been my friend. I suppose time is a friend to no one really. Now it is a huge source of stress. Where did the time go? I don't have enough time in a day to get my work done. I've wasted my time relaxing when I could have been getting something done!

The jobs that "typical" woman took on like that of a secretary, office receptionist, or telephone operator were a terrible fit for me. I wish I would have known before I painfully took on this type of work that I would have been better suited doing something vastly different.

My clumsy, often overloaded, self was terrible working in the service industry where the environment was loud, fast paced, and required multiple customer interactions simultaneously. Although I did significantly better working as a bank teller, where I only had to deal with one customer at a time, working fairly independently, I still was unable to keep the schedule required. To make matters worse, being a stickler for the rules, I had no ability or tolerance for short-cuts; therefore, did not make any friends, but did make many enemies amongst co-workers and supervisors alike.

Being a "know-it-all" and a "stickler" for the rules, did not afford you any leniency when you experience difficulties. No one would go to bat for me when I was staring another termination in the face because of being late—again.

It was never my intention to have, nor did I understand, why I had this type of reputation. I only expected others to play by the rules, the written rules, the ones in black and white that I could fully comprehend. Didn't they understand that those were the only concrete rules that I had to cling to?

I was not opposed to doing things differently because I wanted my own way, or because I was a "know-it-all". I had tremendous difficulty with change, and rearranging the way things were done, especially if I had been taught to do them a certain way. It was very much the same as my first day of kindergarten. The way I learned, or did it the first time, was the way that it stuck, immovable, set in stone; the ONLY correct way.

Clearly my weak central coherence (missing the whole, getting lost in the details), sensory overload, and rigid thinking were hindering my ability to be successful in the adult working world. But was my difficulty with theory of mind becoming a hindrance as well?

Even looking back now I can't find some of the signals and sign posts that I missed along the way. Why would a private investigator want to take a young girl under his wing anyway? Yes—I was incredibly interested in Forensic Science, even though I could not make it through the schooling required for the profession, and I loved the idea of police and undercover work. So when the opportunity arose to take work as an undercover investigator, posing as customers, waitresses, or bartenders in local pubs in order to uncover employee theft I jumped at the chance.

It was a dream job. I would be able to do detective work, which I loved, and I had plenty of experience as a waitress, a bartender, and not to mention I was a professional at hanging out in bars drinking! This was definitely for me. There were other assignments as well, like spying on ex-husbands in the park and videotaping them with their children for custody hearings. Many times I needed to play the ditzy blonde who couldn't use her camera correctly, or who tripped over the kid's ball falling helplessly giggling into her boyfriend's arms (the other private investigator)—hopelessly clumsy.

Even observing other people's behaviors in the work place looking for theft was a good fit—I thought. I was used to observing people. Given a set of behaviors to watch for—I watched. I fear now though, I may have been the new creepy chick that the boss just hired.

What I did not know, what never crossed my mind was why this investigator would "train" me. Those signs, once again, I missed.

One evening after a long day of video-taping in the park, he dropped me off in front of my apartment. Before I got out of the car, he reached over slipped his hand onto my thigh, and tried to kiss me. What? Where did that come from? Was he crazy?

A slap preceded the door slamming on both the car and on my "dream job".

Chapter Sixteen: Damn That Shiny Armor

I was never more *myself* than when I was six years old—a lively little girl who talked too much, knew too much, spun round and round, and ripped her clothes off to run naked through the streets in comfort. She was still rigid and literal-minded, misunderstanding the world of people around her, but she didn't notice. She was carefree—free to be herself.

Memories are marked with odd, quirky, stimming behaviors, but they were just an expression of herself; the way she saw the world, and did things. That little girl knew what she needed, wanted, and what was comforting to her. The young woman I was becoming could not make the same boast. I was rattled and confused.

Adolescence crept up on me and bound and gagged me when I wasn't looking. Adulthood threatened to choke the life from my soul. My happy stimming behaviors were replaced with mind numbing alcohol. My intelligence was not being fed, and my self-worth began to rely on whose attention I attracted. I was on a downward spiral into the abyss of uncertainty.

I was a weird child, but adults accept even weird children. A weird adult, most especially a woman, no one accepts—not really.

I married when I was twenty-three years old, and by that time believe me when I tell you I felt OLD, way past the age when I felt my life should have already began and hadn't. While my friends were finishing up college degrees, or beginning their careers and settling into lives of their own, I was still floundering around trying to find something that fit me—but *nothing fit me.*

When I first met my husband, I was attending a large church in Brooklyn. It was a Tuesday night in May of 1995. I had just finished taking my physical for the New York City Police Department, and had gone directly to the Tuesday night prayer meeting at church. It had been a long day; I had said many prayers to get me through that physical exam. Everyone should go to church sweaty in a t-shirt and stretchy pants.

On our way out of the building I saw him, I don't remember very much else about what was going on around me—damn that shiny armor; here we go again.

He was the complete opposite of me. Dark eyes to contrast my blue eyes, brown hair starkly different than my light blonde, his nose and lips were full, mine pointed and thin, and his olive skin made my marshmallow complexion glow. I don't know how we met really, I just remember looking at him. He was talking; I wasn't listening.

When it was time to leave I offered him a ride home in a car that a student of mine lent me for the week. I was working at Arthur Murray Dance Studios in Manhattan at the time, but was getting ready to leave that job because the next police academy class would be beginning in the end of June. Law enforcement, police work, forensics, investigations—that was where my interest really was, where my heart always lay.

Maybe it was the idea of justice, that naïve belief in the system—good vs. evil; right vs. wrong. That has always been at the core of my being, a passionate morality, a clear distinction between right and wrong; where lines were crisp, and there were no shady grey areas.

He accepted my ride home versus making the long trek from church to his apartment. I am proud to report that he was nothing but a gentleman, and in fact, would you believe he got out of the car, thanked me for the ride, said good-night, and began to walk away from the car!

I sat there slightly shell-shocked.

Beep, Beep. B-b-beep. BEEP.

He hadn't expected me to start honking that horn.

So what happened when I honked that horn at the handsome stranger that I had just given a lift home? He nearly jumped out of his skin.

"You have a phone number?" I yelled to him still half across the street.

Stunned he walked back to the car. "Um, Uh, ya," he stumbled over his words, and put his hands inside his jacket.

"Oh, don't worry. Here—I have a pen." I was prepared.

I wish I could say that it was magical from there—love at first sight, but that would be a lie. Of course on my part, the thing had been decided. I was marrying this one. He was handsome, polite, and genuinely nice to women.

He was the kind of man who opens doors and pulls out chairs, which was a huge change from the bar hopping fools to whom I'd become accustomed. The problem, however, was that he was nice to women. I guess it is a rare commodity to have someone go out of their way to make you feel good, to act like they care about you and your feelings as a person.

There were many things about the two of us that clashed immediately. He was non-committal, had too many "friends", and was the chatty social butterfly. Everyone knew Mark, everyone smiled at him, talked to him—especially the girls. If there was a woman within twenty feet of that man they gravitated to him and it drove me nuts.

Not only did he attract too much attention from woman, it was insincere attention, the kind of attention that I am incapable of giving. Flattery and lies are not a way of being nice—to me lies are flat out the opposite. Lies and flattery to stroke a man's ego to get something you desire in return is not sincere—it's deceitful. I simply cannot tell you that you look great, wonderful, and awesome on days that you do not.

Despite all of these challenges, I was convinced he was the one for me. To tell you the truth, I don't even know what it was that convinced me, but I can say that I knew it almost immediately. The problem was he didn't. He wanted his freedom, his "friends", and his roaming. That—was unacceptable. All his "friends" were female, either current or past dating partners—utterly unacceptable.

For a time we stopped seeing each other, but I didn't see anyone else. In my mind and heart I was wholly committed even if we were apart. After all, how could I say that I loved someone, and be with another? To me, that concept is completely foreign. So I patiently waited for him to come to his senses.

It took two years and two months for him to put a wedding band on my finger. There are some ideas that I get into my head, which in turn get stuck in stone, that turn out to be a good things.

In the two years I'd known my husband prior to our wedding I worked as a dance instructor for Arthur Murray Dance Studies in Manhattan, tried to get in the police academy, worked at a law firm, started a Multi-level Marketing (MLM) business, took a part-time night job in a Brooklyn dance studio, and worked as an Administrative Assistant for a limousine company. Each time either leaving my job for something I perceived as better, or being let go because I failed to maintain a schedule for any length of time.

When I began a job, I was always a superstar. I could focus more intently than any other employee, learn faster, and get more accomplished—until I became overwhelmed. I remained unable to sustain these activities with any degree of competency for an extended period of time. Depending on the work involved *extended* could have meant months, weeks, or mere days.

Life was beginning to once again to become complicated. My one friend (at the time), moved half-way across the country a few months before my wedding. I was left to plan and look forward to my new life seemingly alone. I felt sad, lonely, lost and confused. I had my husband of course, who was rapidly taking that one friend place in my life, but the transition was difficult. He didn't really understand me, in fact, I really didn't understand myself.

For someone on the autism spectrum finding a good fit in a job is tremendously important, as we take much of our self-worth and identity from what we do. More importantly though, I believe, is recognizing when you indeed do have a good fit, and sticking with it. I was not very good at either. Sticking with things was never my strong suit, not unless it was something I was intensely passionate about—a special interest. When I was very young baseball held my attention for many years.

My obsession with baseball was rapidly taken over by dancing. Dancing up until this point was probably my longest running special interest. I began dancing in elementary school, and continued on throughout my early twenties. Although, there were times that other interests even pushed that to the back burner for a while.

Only in hindsight can I now see which of these jobs fit me, and which did not. For the most part, most were *not* good fits, but there was one job that was a better fit than most.

I landed a job as an Executive Administrative Assistant in a small limousine company. The title, however, is misleading. The company was small, and I indeed was the administrative assistant to the CEO, which would have been a terrible job for me in a regular company. But in this company, the job entailed mostly working with the comptroller, and tinkering with accounting software.

I learn to work computer programs quickly, so I was able to navigate any of the company's programs with little to no training. All I needed to do was open a program and tinker with it for a little while in order to be able to use it. I did not have to answer telephones, or work with other staff. I was in a unique position in the company; I mostly worked alone or with the accountant. It was a good fit.

Being a small company in Brooklyn, the job didn't pay very much, but at least there was no dress code. I was able to come to work anyway I chose—jeans were common attire. Additionally, the office was close to my home, about a 3 minute drive, and I could pretty much make my own hours—within reason. I was not penalized for being late; I loved the work, and was left to do it. Best of all—my job didn't require me to talk to anyone.

Looking back I should have stayed there, at least for a little longer than I did. I was newly married, and finances were tight so I began to look for other opportunities—ones that paid more money. I landed a job in Manhattan as a receptionist; the pay was better but not exceedingly so. Still I was moving up in the world, and going to work in the city reasoning that this position was just a stepping stone within the company.

What a mistake! Money does not compensate for misery.

For starters, the job required me to be on a train at 7:00 a.m. in order to make it to my office before 9:00 a.m. My new husband and I lived almost at very end of the "B" line in Brooklyn, near Bay 50th street. The end of the line was only one stop further, where you would reach Coney Island. From that stop to my office took in excess of one and a half hours. What was I thinking?

The first couple of weeks went off without a hitch. It was new; I was on top of getting dressed in business attire, doing my hair, putting on make-up and heels and leaving the house. Might I add at this point that I HATE business attire, priming my hair, and cannot stand the feel of make-up on my face. I suppose it was only a matter of time until I could not stand wearing it any longer and my appearance at work became hairier by the day.

I was exhausted—all the time. There was not enough hours in the day to work, commute, and sleep, there just wasn't. I could barely open my eyeballs in the mornings and drag myself out of the house. Despite my exhaustion, my brain has always worked best when I first open my eyes in the morning. That is the time of the day when I have all my thoughts, dreams, plans, and inspirations. I suspect it is the time of the day I can function best because no one has yet pissed me off.

I was intensely interested in business and finance, real estate and mortgage rates. I loved to talk about ideas, investment property and passive income (a passion of mine), which my husband did not understand or care about. I used to chat his ear off in the mornings while I got ready for work, but he was able to get away from me quickly because he needed to catch his train. Now, however, I rode the train alongside of him, and there was no escape.

Being married only a short time, less than two months; I was overjoyed to spend time talking his ear off on our extremely long commute. He, on the other hand, kept trying to find ways to get me to shut up. He repeatedly told me that it was too early in the morning to talk about finances while his eyes glazed over; I continued to ramble.

As it became more difficult to get out of bed in time, and get out of the house, he began threatening to leave without me. After all, if he waited for me, he too would be late for work. I took it personally. He tried to get me to stop rambling on and on about things he couldn't care less about ALL the way to the city; I tried; I couldn't. He opened his book; I kept talking. He put headphones on; I got angry.

The new job was making me sick. Truly, physically sick.

That's right; I didn't mention what my exact job duties entailed. I was one of three front desk receptionists working behind a circular reception desk—the first people you see when you walk into the company. This particular company was a head-hunting agency, and I actually got the job when I submitted a resume for them to place me somewhere. Since there was a receptionist opening, I was placed right within the company.

Greeting people—first problem.

In addition to the meet & greet responsibilities, I was required to wear a headset and answer a non-stop switchboard the entire day. In the midst of talking to visitors, I needed to simultaneously talk on the phone, answer questions, and transfer phone calls. I rarely got it right, often forgetting who the caller wanted to speak to, or what they just told me their names were. The two other receptionists were chatty pattys. I hated the office politics, the ridiculous drama, and the gossip, so I spent most of the day not speaking to them at all—if I was able avoid it.

Music blared in the background, phones rang, and hundreds of calls routed themselves into my headset interrupting every possible thought I tried to grab hold of. This job was NOT a good fit, in fact, it was awful.

The office manager took pity on me and allowed me to work on a special project in the accounting department for a few days. I did too good of a job and finished my project early, damn it, which only led to me going back to my own desk faster.

Nights became sleepless and tearful, followed by mornings when I was sick to my stomach. I developed gastrointestinal problems, and after an endoscopy was diagnosed with Irritable Bowel Syndrome (IBS).

I was beginning to have difficulty functioning at all. I dreaded mornings, and dreaded heading out to the train station to head to that job even more. I continued to feel exhausted all the time, and was not enjoying my new found stomach issues.

It was at my second doctor's appointment that my physician proclaimed, "You are depressed."

I described my sensitivity to the sounds and lights in my office, my inability to keep two thoughts in my head at the same time, and difficulty staying on a schedule. I discussed my sheer panic at the prospect of meeting and greeting people all day long, or having to keep a headset on over my ears. There was never any explanation given for my "symptoms".

Here—take this little blue pill every morning, and this one, and this one, and this one….

Medication for my stomach, for depression, for inflammation, for pain…I left the pharmacy with a bag full.

The first time I took Zoloft I saw little blue monkeys.

The doctor handed me a stack of prescriptions and sent me on my way, never giving any indication what I would feel like the next day when I obediently took my medications as directed.

I arrived at work the following morning—late—with an extra bag that was full of prescriptions. I hadn't taken any before I left the house because I was running late, and some said, "Take with food". I figured that I would take my medications when I arrived at the office, after picking up a cup of tea and a buttered roll from the street vendor.

Two hours later I had to go home. The room was spinning, I was nauseous, and I had a tremendous amount of difficulty keeping my eyes open! What did they put in these things?

I called my husband who was working uptown at the time, and told him I was going home. I called him again when I found myself in the subway scared to get on the train because the little blue monkeys were looking at me!

He met me at the subway where I was frozen in place, and then got me home. That is where I remained for the next couple days in bed. When I returned to work after my "illness", I was fired—again. Thank goodness!

Within a few weeks my IBS resolved itself, and I was no longer "depressed", but I was once again, unemployed. Oh—and I no longer took any more of those *little blue pills*.

Chapter Seventeen: Adult Autism Hurts

Childhood was fleeting. I'd entered the adult world, but try as I might to tread water the current continued to pull me under. The world around me was changing—swiftly. Old friends were growing, beginning careers, and starting families while I floundered. Everyone had a direction, a dream, a focus—not me. I seemed to tumble where the wind tossed me, never truly recovering before the next gust sent me sailing again.

Yes—adult autism hurts.

It hurt when I raced to my car to make my next class, and lost my footing, tumbling down the side of a grassy hill, right after it rained, and rose covered with mud dripping from my hair. I was a real sight in my next class; that was a memorable entrance.

It hurt when my high heel got wedged in between the elevator shaft and the elevator platform causing me to nearly break my leg and get hit in the head with the closing door on my way down to the floor. I worked the rest of that day with a limp, broken shoe, and torn stockings.

It hurt when I fell into the only hole in the street, the one everyone else slid over with ease. And when I slipped on the black ice and landed under the parked car.

It was painful when I took one step, and then tumbled end over end down half a flight of stairs and somehow ended up with both legs up on the wall. It is a good thing that townhouse was carpeted, it cushioned my fall.

I was not as lucky when I tripped over my own feet in front of my Brooklyn apartment, and flew down the concrete steps. The only thing that saved my face was the cheesecake it landed in.

Adult autism burned when I pulled my coffee mug out of the microwave, applying a little too much strength, and sent the scolding liquid raining down on top of me—or worse the times when my fingers failed to hold on to the mug altogether and it crashed into kitchen wall.

It hurt when I misjudged the weight of the door entering the deli up the street, and I crashed face-first into the glass, and when I pulled at the pizzeria door a little too hard sending myself sailing backwards.

It hurt when my butt hit the floor and my groceries spilled out all over the sidewalk. Or, when I pulled at the cabinet door in my kitchen too hard smacking myself in the head with it.

It hurt last summer when I fell, face first, into a one foot kiddy pool on vacation—holding my son.

But most of all—as an adult with autism, it hurts to feel completely and utterly alone.

So why can I not keep my feet underneath me, or apply the correct amount of pressure when lifting an object? Why do I walk into a room like an elephant in a china shop, or send the milk container flying across the room when it is *too light?* In a word—proprioception.

What is proprioception?

Proprioception refers to one's own perceptions. It an unconscious perception of movement and spatial orientation controlled by nerves within the body.

Our proprioceptive system allows us to locate our bodies in space, to be aware of where our arms and legs are in relation to one another, as well as, where they begin and where they end. Proprioception helps us perceive the outside world, telling us whether our bodies are moving or sitting still.

This system helps us perceive the amount of force needed to complete a task, and then allows us to apply it appropriately. It helps us measure and perceive distances, allowing us to move through our world without crashing into everything around us.

Child and adults with autism often have difficulty with proprioception and very well may just be the thing that goes bump in the night…and the day, and at work, and in the streets. Poor proprioception may likely be responsible for those many bruises, skinned knees, and torn stockings that plague our days.

It can be difficult to explain how we, those with Asperger's Syndrome/Autism, can be so clumsy in our day to day activities, but so adept when we are intently focused. I spent a great deal of my life dancing. I could dance with the grace of a swan, and fall down steps on my way off the stage.

I believe the difference is the intensity of our focus. We can, for a short period of time, intensely focus on crossing a balance beam to get to the other side. However, it is impossible to sustain that level of focus in all our activities 24 hours per day. I am sure that I would never fall down again, if I could focus on every step I took to the exclusion of everything else—with no distractions and no interruptions.

While a "normal" person unconsciously perceives and is aware of each step they take, an autistic person must think about and focus consciously to perceive what comes naturally to others. If I do not physically watch my feet taking each step, I wind up on the ground.

"Alone. Yes, that's the key word, the most awful word in the English tongue. Murder doesn't hold a candle to it and hell is only a poor synonym."
— Stephen King

I should have been happy, but I was hurting.

I couldn't hold down a job. I was sick for no apparent reason. I was newly married, but feeling completely alone.

I never had very much in common with my friends to begin with, and now that I was married and they were not—we had even less in common. To make matters worse, I was quickly discovering I had nothing in common with my new husband either. What the hell is wrong with me?

Communication in our house was dwindling down to nothing. My brain was wide-awake first thing in the morning, and wanted to ramble on-and-on about whatever interested me at the time. My husband had no interest in *my interests*, and I had no interest in his.

What were his interests anyway? I truly don't know. Maybe because it didn't interest me, it didn't register, or maybe he had no interests I deemed worthwhile at all. I absolutely hated walking around in the city—destination, no-where. I did not enjoy shopping, let alone window shopping. I found no purpose in looking around at things we may someday want to buy, when I had no money to buy it now. If I went to a store, it was to purchase something I needed, and even then I usually was not happy about it.

Mornings were not my husband's favorite time of the day, but by the time nightfall arrived I was too wiped out to think. I had nothing left in me to talk about, nothing that was important to me. If I'd had a particularly over-stimulating or stressful day, there was no way I was listening what happened in his. I just couldn't do it. I couldn't listen to him ramble on about what went on in the office, or focus on his feelings.

Listening to meaningless nonsense about people I did not know or care about made me want to gouge my eyeballs out—or worse, his.

"No one else's views have any validity in your eyes," he said.

"Because they are wrong."

That was all there was to it, if the other person's opinion, idea, or view was wrong, it was wrong. There is nothing in the world that was going to change my mind; nothing that was going to make something that is wrong, right—nothing.

Besides, isn't that the point—it was my point of view he continually invalidated. He could not understand what I was saying; therefore, it had no validity. He blocked out my words, shut out my opinions, and cut off my spirit. Maybe I had made a mistake, maybe I was wrong, maybe this guy was all wrong for me.

I had no one. No one to talk to, at least that is the way I felt. No one to hold on to, or who would hold tightly back. No one to tell me everything was going to be all right. No one to say, yes, me too, I know how you feel—No one.

Chapter Eighteen: Year One of Marriage Sucked

Within the first four months, he lost his job, started working two jobs (day and night), and then lost those two as well. I left a job that suited me for a "better one," messed that one up, and got impossibly sick because of it. By our first Christmas, we were both unemployed.

He looked for work; I looked for something else I could "do with myself."

In the winter of 1998, we bought our first computer, which is when I discovered I enjoyed tinkering with it, and I enjoyed typing. Maybe it is that repetitive soothing motion it offers. I purchased a learn to type program, and obsessively taught myself to type…40 wpm…60 wpm…125 wpm!

There was more running around my beady little brain than just typing. I was taking a home medical transcriptionist course.

Medical terminology came easily to me; the structures of the words were formed logically, many times rooted in Latin.

The course took me only three months in total to complete. Now, I had a skill. I set out immediately to find another job. A week later, I was working as a medical secretary, and transcriptionist for an Osteoporosis Center.

The Center had two offices in Brooklyn; one downtown, and the other in Bensonhurst where I lived. Perfect, no long train rides into Manhattan. It lasted three weeks.

"We are going to have to let you go," the office manager told me on Friday morning when I arrived at work.

I didn't understand. I was not late; I'd arrived on time each day. My reports were produced on time, and accurately. What was the problem?

"You made a personal call from work, which is against our policy."

"What policy? Am I three years old that I am not allowed to call home to see if I needed to pick up a gallon of milk on my way home?" I said.

"And, you were rude to patients."

"Rude to patients? When was I rude to patients?"

Again, I hopped on the train to make the trip back to our small apartment with my head hung. I'd lost yet another job, and this time, I did not even know why.

In the late 1990's working from home was a dream. No one I knew actually did it, and others thought I was crazy for thinking that I could make money without going to work in a job. This never made any sense to me. Having a job, working for someone else, making someone else rich—not only was not appealing, but was illogical. Of course, I was the only one in our house to see it this way.

Determined, if nothing else, I would figure out a way. The one sure-fire way to get me to do *anything* is to tell me I can't; it could not be done—maybe it was just stubbornness. Stubbornness that paid off.

I began typing medical reports from home for a transcription company. I worked as an independent contractor acquiring all of my jobs over the telephone (Dictaphone) system. When completed, the reports were transmitted over the internet directly into the dictating hospitals' computer systems. No getting dressed in the mornings, trudging through the streets in the cold, or dealing with people in an office—I worked completely alone.

I had succeeded at something finally, and my confidence in myself was increasing. I had done what everyone said I could not; I made more money "not working" than going to work. That is how family, friends and neighbors saw me, as someone who did not work because I did not leave the house to go to an office—how ridiculous. I worked. In fact, I worked harder for myself, longer hours, and only got paid for production.

There were no paid sick days, no holidays, or vacation time. If I did not work, I did not get paid—simple as that, and it was fine by me. But to say I did not work, that was insulting. Other people could have a lazy day and simple show up at work and do the bare minimum—I could not.

My new found wings grew only to be clipped, nailed to the ground, and stomped upon. I thought things at home were getting better; I thought we were communicating; I thought everything was fine.

I never could understand the need to get out of bed at 4 a.m. to tinker on the internet before work, and then complain you're tired and don't get enough sleep. I mean—that makes no sense, stay in bed.

Morning after morning my husband would get up before the sun to hop on the computer, and load up AOL. I didn't understand it, but I didn't question it—why would I?

Internet pornography crept into my life. I didn't want it, I didn't invite it, and I never saw it coming. What began as conversations in chat rooms escalated to pictures, videos, and illicit chats.

My breath caught in my throat. I tried to speak but could say nothing as I stared at the computer screen. Message after message from women wanting to chat popped up in the right-hand corner of the screen. Now I know why he was reluctant, panicked even, to give me his password so that I could change a setting on our computer.

I could barely hear over the blood rushing through my ears and the thumping in my chest. I was frozen, my butt glued to my chair, but my fingers still worked—enough to dial the bastard's work number anyway.

I screamed, I flung things, I cursed, I cried, and then—I left.

Two months and plenty of counseling later I found out I was pregnant with my first son. Again, life was changing—fast.

I was thrilled—over the moon. I have always wanted children, a family, a home filled with fun, love, and peace. I longed for the ideal romanticized family full of smiles and laughter. My husband was sorry; all was forgiven; life was grand.

For a short time I rejoiced, and then grandpa died.

He didn't look well; he didn't feel well. Grandma set her tea aside, dropped me off at home, and drove Grandpa straight to the emergency room. That was the last time I saw him. My heart hurt more than it had ever hurt before, but I couldn't show it—not with other people around.

I arrived to the funeral parlor early to sit with him alone. I sat there just staring, no tears, just blank, numb. My best friend moved away, my grandpa was gone, my belly was full of life, but I was empty. It was time to run.

I stood staring at the house—my house with the sun streaming through the trees.

I was born here, and part of me died here. The haunting echoes of my childhood lingered in the halls. I could hear it; run from it. I bit my trembling bottom lip determined to hold back the tears.

My stomach tightened when I looked at the empty rooms, my vanquished memories. The ones I'd thrust off to someplace new—away from where the air was infused with freshly baked semolina from the bakery up the street. Away from where lunch was routinely a Sicilian slice from the pizzeria around the corner, or thinly sliced prosciutto and fresh mozzarella still hot from the vat, spread across crisp Italian bread. There would be no salmerias or delis in the Mississippi delta—no fresh baked cookies, Italian pastries or ices in the summertime.

I took a last look at the two-story brick house I'd grown up in, and the children running through the open Johnny pump, and then at the taxi waiting at the curb. The baby wiggled in my arms, as if he knew more than I, at only eight weeks of age. One tear escaped from my eye.

Grandpa had stood in the same place that I did, in the shade of the dogwood tree. He'd worn a smile from ear to ear when he overheard the news. Three weeks later he was gone. I tucked a sonogram picture into his pocket as he slept in his mahogany casket. That was the beginning of the end.

My arms trembled as I looked up at the dogwood tree—my tree. Grandpa planted that tree ten years earlier, right in front of the house. He tore up the patch of concrete himself and then built a white fence around his gift. "See, a tree *can* grow in Brooklyn," he said when he showed it to me.

My husband's arm wrapped around my shoulder, "You ready to go?"

I nodded, and then watched him put the last of the suitcases in the back of the cab. The sounds of soft sobs drew closer behind me. I couldn't speak, my chest hurt, and my feet felt cemented to the stoop.

My father's tears always turned his eyes the brightest of blues. That day my eyes were gray. I knew I had to do this; a new life awaited us—a new job, a new house, a new baby, a new place. It was my idea after all.

The sun shone through the trees, but days this bright should not be so sad. *Deep breaths, I can do this, I can say good-bye to this place.*

Chapter Nineteen: A Disconnected Mom

I sat in our three bedroom, two bath rented home in the Mississippi Delta rocking back and forth on the edge of my sofa, holding my temples as the baby screamed. Dishes piled up in the sink, mail on the dining room table, toys lay sprawled across the living room floor, and piles of VHS tapes sat in front of the hearth.

Clothes were heaped in the corner of the bedroom—piled as high as the unmade bed while the diaper pail overflowed. The curtains remained drawn to close out the light, to shut out the world.

He screamed, he screamed, and he screamed some more. If my son's eyes were open he was screaming—even if they were shut he cried in his sleep. No one could explain it; not his pediatrician, or the Emergency Room staff; not my friends, or family back home; no one.

"He has colic."

That was their answer—for an entire year!

"I was never so happy to have a job in my life," my husband said.

Of course he was happy; he got to leave the house.

One of the bedrooms was converted into a modest office with an unstable desk, outdated computer, dial-up internet connection, and a kitchen chair. I transcribed medical reports for Queens Hospital in New York, transmitting my work over the internet. At least I was still able to make money from home.

I spent many nights trying to get those reports typed, and woke in the morning drooling on my keyboard. The remaining nights I cried myself to sleep. Working from home was great when I was free to hop in the car and go have tea with Grandma, but as a house hostage in a strange land, it was devastating.

I was wholly disconnected from my life. Disconnected from everyone and everything I knew. Far away from lunches with Grandma, away from my parents, my brothers, and all my childhood friends. Taking this autistic girl far from her home and family was a very bad idea. Everything changed when I left home; parts of me were lost never again to be recovered.

Moving away from everything I knew, and becoming a mother for the first time highlighted how different I was from other women.

I suppose I didn't notice it as much at home because I was connected to people. I was satisfied being odd, weird, a little different—just like my Grandmother. Everyone who knew her knew me, and that made me seem—not quite as odd.

Maybe had I stayed, she would have known what to do about my baby's screaming, or been there to tell me that I was normal after all. Maybe she could have just made me a cup of tea—that always made me feel better.

Surrounded by proper southern women who felt the need to tell me how they would not let my kid get away with this or that, or how he would eat what they put in front of him did not help me. Other women ran their household's with ease. Homes were immaculate, cabinets organized, bills paid, children fed, bathed, and in bed by seven o'clock.

Not a hair on their heads were out of place, while mine stuck out in every direction. Their make-up was applied flawlessly, they never left the house without putting on their face. The best I accomplished most days was slipping out of my pajamas, and into my sweats, or a pair of jean shorts and a t-shirt. My idea of hair being neat was slicking it back into a ponytail. If the little fly away hairs stayed stuck down, I was good.

I was sinking—fast; drowning in my own guilt and confusion while trying desperately to take a breath of sanity. There was none to be found. There was something very wrong; surely, going back home would fix it.

We moved back to Brooklyn just before my oldest son's third birthday. He'd already proved to be an interesting child—extremely picky about what he would wear, or eat. He spoke a million miles a minute to any adult who would listen to him.

For an entire year, the only things he ate were brown and serve sausages, and buttered crackers. It didn't matter how many people said he needed to eat his veggies, he was not going to eat them. Sausage and buttered crackers—that was it.

If I tried to put a pair of blue jeans on him, he screamed and tore them from his body. Blue fireman pants were all he would wear. Blue fireman pants were blue active pants, the kind that were water resistant. We owned at least ten pairs of the same pants. Making him look like he had more than one outfit was not worth the meltdowns. I endured the stares.

When the screaming let up just after his first birthday we moved on to him being the vomit kid. He didn't vomit because of odors as I had when I was a child. He produced projectile vomit anytime we were in the car. Two blocks from the house was usually as far as I could get without incident. To this day, he sits in the car with his head hung out the window like a puppy knowing the inevitable vomit is coming.

There were perpetual ear infections, asthma, allergies, and general madness. He was not an easy child.

When we moved back to New York, he stopped speaking. Daycare workers could not speak to him so we enrolled him in the Montessori school. There his teacher complained of not being able to understand him, and that he did not get along with the other children. "Maybe Montessori is not a good fit for him," she said.

My husband and I mistakenly thought that his lack of speech was the teacher's fault, or because of moving, or the difference in accents. It never occurred to us that it could be anything more. Doctors, parents, and teachers missed autism in me, and I missed it in him.

We enrolled our son in a private Christian school, where he started pre-K. From the first day of school every morning was the same. I dropped him off, and he screamed, cried, kicked, yelled, and held on to me for dear life. I felt like an awful mother.

Less than a month later, his teacher wanted him "evaluated" because she could not handle him. She lost him one day, and the assistant principal found him roaming the halls. How did she not see him leave her room? She lost him another day because she forgot he went into the bathroom an hour earlier, and never came out.

The classroom was small, and the restroom was inside the room—a single person restroom much like the one we had at home. He loved to go into that bathroom and stay there locking himself in—or was he locking his teacher out?

When he was not hiding out in the bathroom, he was sitting under the table by himself. He refused to sit with the other children, and his teacher accused him of not paying attention. He was paying attention because when I asked him any question about what they did in school that day, he had the correct answer. He just refused to sit with the other children.

I balked at the idea of an evaluation for my child when his teacher was clearly incompetent, but in the end I went ahead and made the appointment.

My son was taken into a room with ten other children, all ages 6 and 7—my son was 4! He sat under the table, tinkered with his shoes, and basically ignored everything that was going on. This "group session" lasted 45 minutes, at the end of which the doctor pronounced that my son has ADHD and needs medication.

"I don't think so!"

That doctor never spoke to my son. He only said, "As you can see he could not sit still." Hell, I could not sit still!

It was mid-December and I was pregnant with my second child, when I got a phone call from the school. My son had locked himself in the vice-principal's office and would not open the door, or come out. His teacher sent him to spend the day in the office because she refused to have him in her classroom until I consented to putting him on medication. That was his last day of Pre-K.

I thought I could go back; I thought I could return to the place I loved, to the people I loved, and everything would be better. But—in life you can only move forward, you cannot go back.

I did not perceive the passage of time. When I returned home everything was different. My grandfather's glue had dried up and my family fell apart. Fifty years of memories sold to the highest bidder— the home I grew up in and loved was no longer home. Bars covered the windows that strange faces now peered out from. How can so much change in so few years?

Grandma sold the house after we moved away—it was my fault because I didn't stay.

Although everything was different, many things remained the same. I found myself employed, unemployed, and re-employed again. We struggled with finances, as did everyone around us, but my ability to cope with the added stress was dwindling. Going back was not the way I dreamed it would be.

It seems as soon as I am in a new situation, I begin looking for ways out of it. Searching for greener grass, reaching for what is out of reach, looking for what I was unable to define. A change of location, job, and friends was always the perceived answer—and it was always the wrong one.

Looking back through enlightened eyes, ones that now filter life through the lens of autism; I can clearly see how I take longer to learn from where I've been than others. The difficulty and often inability to generalize information, and to apply it to future situations becomes apparent.

I told myself that the disconnection and loneliness that I felt when we moved to the Mississippi Delta was because of its location. It could not have possible been that my loneliness came from being disconnected from all that was familiar to me, from all my friends, and from all my family. Surely, moving to a cheaper cost of living location would provide more stability and happiness in my life.

Happiness—an indefinable state, the elusive shadow I continued to pursue.

I've suffered from depression on and off for years, but if I found new places to live (I thought) I could keep it at bay. If I kept moving I could stay one step ahead of the depression that followed me; the depression that stalked me, threatening to cover me with darkness and suffocate the life out of me. If I just keep going, moving, changing, searching, I could outrun it—but I could not. The dark cloud that pursued me caught up; it ran faster than I did.

It caught up with me in a new place, a new home, a new town, in the countryside. It took me over in the living room, at work, and on the front porch. Depression sapped my energy, my ambition, my dreams, and my very will to take another breath.

I fear depression—intensely. It is by far the most painful ailment I have ever faced. It is the thing that slammed into me, ran me over repeatedly, and then kicked me in the head when I was down. I struggled for change, for understanding, to figure out what was "wrong" with me—no one knew. Or at least, they didn't guess correctly.

Now overwhelmed by new surroundings, a new workplace, and new people with whom I didn't fit, my carefully constructed façade began to crumble. I became lost in my own world more often, trying to complete tasks at work, but becoming quickly overwhelmed I lost track of my hours—of my days.

Headaches began; the kind that I needed to rock through while holding my temples. The noises all joined together—the humming of the florescent light bulbs, the sounds of people talking, the phones ringing. I heard the noises but could not stop them from running together. Voices blended together to the point that I had difficulty understanding the words that were being spoken to me.

My own speech became jumbled, as I struggled to find the correct phrases, to pull from the correct database of words. I stuttered, until finally I had no words at all. Tears fell, my breath quickened, and the world spun. My heart raced so quickly it felt like it would explode—like I would die.

Chapter Twenty: Diagnosis Crazy

Whenever I have difficulty articulating a problem, I write a list, an explanation, a description. The written word has always served me well, and allowed me to open myself up to the world when my verbal words have failed me.

After several doctor's visits, I was still having trouble telling him all that was concerning to me. My clumsiness, my forgetfulness, my sensitivities to light, sounds, textures, and tastes— the overheating after showers, the water that felt like shards of glass hitting my skin.

I tried to explain my loss of speech, my loss of words—but of course, my speech failed me. The more stressful the situation, the more mixed up my vocabulary became, so I faxed him a letter—a seven page letter detailing my concerns. Soon after I was sent for a psych evaluation.

My doctor decided that I was depressed and gave me anti-depressants. I couldn't really argue with that first impression because

I definitely was depressed. I was again lost and alone—disconnected, and now overwhelmed as well.

The spinning world that caused my heart to race, my brow to sweat, and me to hyperventilate, was diagnosed as panic attacks. The anti-anxiety medication Xanax was added to my anti-depressants.

I learned after the fact that the FDA warns that if panic attacks begin or get worse while taking Xanax, that the medication should be discontinued immediately. My panic increased to the point that I was fearful of leaving the house alone. The doctor doubled the dosage.

The medication madness did not end with anti-anxiety and anti-depressant drugs. Although, doctors tried to contribute my neurological symptoms to depression, depression simply did not explain my sensory processing issues. I was sent to a neurologist for evaluation to rule-out Multiple Sclerosis (MS).

CT-scans, MRI's, myelograms, spinal taps, a femoral muscle biopsy, a sural nerve biopsy, blood work, and three specialist later, revealed degenerative disk disease and peripheral neuropathies, which could not be explained. Back pain was something I had always lived with and because of my hypo-sensitivity to pain, I rarely complained to a doctor about it. The medications dulled that hypo-sensitivity allowing the pain to hit me full force. Muscle relaxers and pain medications were added to my already long list of medications.

Taking anti-depressants, anti-anxiety medications, muscle relaxers, and pain killers three times a day made it impossible to do anything—including keeping my eyes open for any amount of time. I began sleeping sixteen hours per day. The solution—they gave me Provigil to wake me in the morning. That stimulant kept me awake for 48 hours; so they added Trazadone, which would help me to sleep.

Anytime there was an issue or a complaint regarding my medications, another was introduced. Within a couple of months I was a walking pharmacy.

I wound up with several different diagnoses, which explained different "symptoms", but none that explained them all. Having executive function impairment the diagnosis of ADHD was added, along with Adderall to help me function. Several other medications such as Cymbalta, and Invega were introduced, and then all this medication quite literally drove me mad.

The combination of medications caused a state of Psychotic Mania, leaving me running around the streets rummaging through people's trash looking for treasure—treasures that I could sell; treasure that was going to make me rich. I was completely out of my mind.

The mania brought along with it one other thing—another diagnosis, bi-polar disorder.

I wish I could tell you more about this period in time, about how and why I decided to start flushing the medications instead of ingesting them. But the truth is, most of what I can convey is second hand. Events relayed to me in the aftermath of this destruction. I have little to no memory of this time period, which lasted almost three full years.

I have no memory of my children's birthdays, no memories of Christmas mornings, no memories of family vacations—they are gone—lost forever.

The misdiagnoses caused doctors to prescribe medications I did not need. The medications had unexpected effects on me, which were then treated with yet more medications, until I was out of my mind. None of the diagnoses was correct; none of them explained what was "wrong" with me; none of them could.

In the end, when the my neurologist was at a loss to understand the myriad of complex symptoms that I now know to be all traits of my Autism Spectrum Disorder, or side-effects of multiple medications, he determined that it was just *"all in my head."* I was crazy.

There were days that I accepted my life would never amount to anything. I was crazy; professionals declared it. All my neurological issues, my sensitivities, my inflexible processing was a product if my imagination. Maybe I was just a lazy horrible person looking for an excuse for her behavior—a reason to keep everyone away.

I began to pity my husband, who was stuck with a crazy wife, and a terrible one at that. My poor children, stuck with a crazy woman for a poor excuse of a mother. It would be better for them if I was just gone, disappeared, vanished into the fog.

A year passed during which time I hardly ever left the house. I began cursing the mornings, and the sun for rising. I rose each day angered that I still drew breath; that I was wasting the air my lungs sucked in. I lived in the deepest darkest depths of hell, where depression lived and my soul died.

No longer having any faith in healthcare professionals, and even less in *mental* healthcare professionals, I was left at the mercy of the dark demon I know as depression.

I began to look at my children, whom I loved more than anything in the world, and wondered how they would remember me— their crazy mother.

What stories would they tell their friends over drinks? Would they only remember a woman who stared into space, lived in her pajamas on the sofa crying while the mess piled up all around her? Would they remember anything else at all?

Life had come to a screeching halt, a stand still. There was no air to breathe, not even a hint of wind to rustle the leaves of the trees—it was dead still. I was numb; I no longer felt anything.

Life was coming apart, crumbling down around me.

I guess something still stirred though—deep in the depths of my mind. Something I did not know what nagging at me, haunting me, awaking my sense of injustice.

Injustice—that is the one thing I cannot live with, the one thing that I cannot accept. The unfairness of the doctor's statements, the idea that it was all in my head, but I felt it acutely. How could that be correct? It didn't make any sense.

All the things they claimed were wrong with me, all the different diagnosis to explain away every symptom—none of it made sense. There must be one thing—one central cause for my pain, *one* explanation.

I pushed these ideas from my conscious thought- focusing instead on myself. The problem must be me, I must try to change, to do something with myself, make something of myself, and find something I can like to do again, something I can enjoy — something I can obsess about because happiness is special interests.

Chapter Twenty-One: Autism Helped Diagnose My Autism

I found my next obsession sitting at my kitchen table with my brother. He was online playing a game of poker. I played poker as a child with my uncles. They taught me how to play, and would allow me to sit with them when my parents went out on Friday nights. Babysitting me was easy—just give me some cards and a stack of chips and I happily played cards with the grown-ups.

Those nights of playing poker in the basement of my grandparent's house with my uncles were a long time ago. I barely remembered how to play; I could not recall all the rules. Wanting to play again, and wanting to beat my brother, I decided it was time to learn again.

One of the diagnostic criteria for Asperger's Syndrome is in a category entitled Restricted Repetitive & Stereotyped patterns of behavior, interests, and activities—an encompassing preoccupation with one or more stereotyped and restricted patterns of interest that is abnormal in either intensity or focus.

I clearly did not fit these criteria. I didn't have any restricted repetitive and stereotyped patterns of behavior. My interests were not abnormal—many people are interested in poker. Many people love playing poker—and some even play poker for a living. Why is my interest abnormal?

In either intensity or focus—still I could not see it. I wanted to learn and the logical way to learn something is to study; so study I did. I've been told that I have an obsession with knowledge, that when I want to learn something I need to know everything about it. This is true, but I could not comprehend why or how this could be considered abnormal. If something was worth doing then I had to do it all the way, or not at all.

I have no middle-ground. If I am going to only half-ass do something, then I am not going to bother doing it at all. So, I began to learn to play poker.

I purchased book after book written by professional poker players. I have an entire bookcase in my master bed room full of poker books; it is my poker library. I subscribed to Bluff and Card Player Magazines, joined several online poker rooms, training sites, and paid for private coaching. I studied cash game, sit-n-go, and tournament strategies.

I played poker every waking hour that I was possibly able. There were times I played for more than 24 hours without taking breaks to eat, sleep, or use the bathroom until I was about to burst. While I played, I watched tournaments on television studying poker pros.

On my television there was always a poker tournament playing. I was either watching the World Series of Poker, the World Poker Tour, or Poker After Dark on NBC. An absence of live programming didn't stop me, I made certain to always have plenty of recorded episodes. When I wasn't playing, which was not very often, or I was not watching live poker on television, I was watching movies about poker. My husband and 13-year old loved "Rounders" with Matt Damon and Ed Norton, and luckily are the types who can watch and re-watch movies over and over again.

I belonged to poker training sites and forums, which saved my husband from at least some of my endless ramblings about poker odds and strategies. My computer software recorded tens of thousands of hands that I physically played allowing me to replay (watch) the games and study what I did that was right or wrong. I reached the point where I could comfortably play ten tables at a time, and keep track of exactly what was happening on each table—as long as you didn't speak to me.

Even when I could not be in the house playing, I brought my poker books and magazines to the pool and sat reading while the boys swam. I was dead serious about playing poker, and if I was going to play, I was going to know what I was doing. I was studying—nothing abnormal about that!

What is so special about special interests?

I can focus for hours and hours on end reading, writing, or playing poker. The rest of the world disappears; I can forget it exists. It calms me, and the stress melts away. When I'm focused on one of my interests, I lose track of time, forget to eat, and am annoyed at even the interruption of needing to use the bathroom.

Interruptions invoke immediate anger. This is not a conscious response. It's my first knee-jerk reaction. I can't control it; anger is just the first response. I can, however, control my reaction to that anger. But make no mistake about it—that is not something that comes naturally *or* easily.

Controlling my immediate reactions is one of those things that are easier said than done.

To other people it is a mystery how I can focus so intently on special interests but have no sustainable focus for anything else. What they don't understand is that being absorbed by my interests is how I decompress.

Focusing on and sustaining life activities…jobs, budgets, housekeeping, etc. takes from me. It is an exhausting struggle; a desperate attempt to tread water while drowning.

Life drains my well. Special interests fill it back up. I need that time, I need that filling, that relaxing, that decompressing, in order to accomplish the other tasks in my life.

My special interests have changed throughout my life, and for a long time I was frustrated by this. It fed the idea that I can never stick with, or complete anything. Now I know that it is *normal* for these intense interests to change, and I try to not feel so bad about myself for putting so much energy into something only to have it lose its awe.

This is the thing about Aspie special interests or obsessions— they may seem abnormal to the Neuro-typical, (those without autism), world both in intensity and focus, but to us they are completely normal. Beyond being normal, our obsessions are positive, empowering, and absolutely necessary.

What some may view as obsessive, odd, weird, abnormal, and troublesome is a necessary part of our happiness. Our interests allow us to decompress, calm down, focus our energy, and gives us a reason to be excited about life—a purpose. An absence of obsessive interest leaves me feeling alone in the darkness.

My poker interest brought me from the depths of my despair and had me looking forward to the next day, the next session.

These special interests can be long-term life-long interests, span several years, as did my obsession with baseball as a child, or be very brief in duration, but they will all have one thing in common: intensity.

The ability of an autistic person to focus so intently and completely on a topic of interest is a gift—one of their super powers. Cultivate, encourage, and cherish these interests because in doing so you are cherishing the autistic person themselves.

Although my poker playing gave me something to focus on, deep inside I still knew there was something missing, something wrong. Something I could neither understand nor put my finger upon--something just beyond my grasp.

I was floating in this life, purposeless and alone searching for some kind of explanation for being me. I had little sense of identity. I saw no one else in my world like me, no one that understood me, that thought like me.

I used to feel special, different and wonderful when I was very young, before the world showed me that everything I thought, said, or did was wrong. I lived in the blissfulness of youth without knowing how the world would not accept me.

Back then there were a precious few who saw the sun rise and set on me, who didn't seek to change me, who only wanted to be a part of me. Those were the people long lost, that I again needed to find. If I could not find them, then I suppose I could create them. If I could not make friends, I could create them upon the blank pages of my computer screen, in my legal pads, in the stories I had bottled up inside.

I could write myself a life; a life that I could live inside the pages of a book without having to interact with the real world around me, with a world who would not accept me the way I am. And so, I began to write. Writing became my new special interest. A special interest that took my life in a direction I never saw coming.

Before I realized that I had absolutely no idea how to construct a story, or how to write properly, I penned an entire novel. Then, I wanted to learn how to do it the right way. The obsession began.

I read book after book on the craft of writing. I was particularly interested in writing fictional stories--novels basically because I could not write anything short, I simply had too much to say and too much trouble letting go of my "friends"--the ones I created on the pages to keep me company.

I enrolled in writing workshops, and decided at 38 years old to make another attempt at college, strictly online, and pursue a bachelor's degree in English. It was this interest, this obsession, this obsessively seeking knowledge that brought me to my Asperger's diagnosis.

I never saw myself. My thoughts, my ideas, the way I did things were unique. There was no one in my life quite like me, except for maybe my grandmother. I never saw myself on the pages of stories, in fictional characters. In fact, I read very little fiction. I read to learn, to research, to study, to gain knowledge--never for entertainment. Life was not entertaining.

Fictional characters left me just as confounded as "real" people. Even fictional people looked nothing like me. That is, until the day I enrolled in a Popular Fiction literature class.

This was a class I was sure I could never enjoy. Reading and studying what was "popular" was never my thing. Actually, I didn't even recognize any of the books on the required reading list. Life in my bubble isolated me from the popular.

Many of those books I would have never picked up to read, not unless I was forced to do so. The definition of popular fiction for the class's purpose was books that struck a chord within society, as well as, within the individual, touching the heart of humanity. The heart of a people I didn't understand and felt I didn't I didn't belong to.

During the last weeks of the class it finally happened. I found myself sprawled out upon the pages, meaning I came across a character that made perfect sense to me, a character whose logic and thought processes were very much like my own. To my chagrin, she confounded the rest of the class.

Class discussions revealed their complete and utter misunderstanding of the character at hand, but I understood her. The character in the book had Asperger's Syndrome.

Up until this point in time, I had never heard the term let alone had any idea it was a form of autism. I didn't connect the dots. It didn't occur to me that there may be a reason I understood her, a reason I felt an odd kinship I'd never before felt.

When my husband read the book he proclaimed, "That's you!" I, being unable to relate one situation to another, to take information and generalize that information did not make the connection; I could not see it. There was simply no way I was autistic.

I suppose the universe was trying to tell me something, because the truth began to stalk me.

For the most part I pushed my similarity to the strange character out of my mind, but my husband was persistent. After doing some research he really felt that I could have Asperger's.

I had to admit that he made a compelling argument, and much of the information he read did sound like I fit the bill. Again, I pushed the thoughts aside.

Two semesters after I took that Popular Fiction class, I did a study on American idioms for an English Language class. Idioms, metaphoric language, figures of speech have always driven me up the wall.

As a child I had a terrible time deciphering the meaning of this language. It made no sense. Meaningless turns of phrases were all it was to me. As I grew I learned by memorizing the meanings of phrases, idioms, mostly by learning the origins of the phrases and explaining to people why their use of said phrase made no sense, which did not make me many friends.

The research for this class' final paper brought me back to Asperger's Syndrome. I began researching how children learn idioms, and often misinterpret their meanings or take the words literally. I had always done this so it was the logical place to start, which is when I stumbled upon it once again.

Very young children and those with autism do not understand idioms. Children, however, grow and learn, but autistic adults often time find these useless turns of phrase confounding. I began to see myself, my thoughts, how my brain worked, in these same autistic adults.

That was twice in the same year I saw reflections of me on the pages of books, and I had no choice but to start searching, to start looking under every rock for the familiar I could never find before.

Another special interest emerged: Autism, Asperger's Syndrome became one of my special interests. To me, that meant I had to learn everything there was to know about it, read every book, every account, every blog entry about and by autistic people. For the first time in my life, I was no longer alone; I was no longer scared; no longer confused. I am autistic, and there are others like me.

The journey, my journey to find myself, to find out what was wrong with me had not come to an end, but to a beginning--to the beginning of my understanding of me.

Less than one month later, I received an official diagnosis.

Chapter Twenty-Two: Grieving My Diagnosis

Denial, anger, blame, tears, and depression—I went through them all before finally accepting my diagnosis.

In the beginning I pushed the signs aside, denied the truth that was trying to flag me down and get my attention. But—I could not deny the facts. I went for neuropsychological testing, and took the AQ (Autism Quotient) and EQ (Empathy Quotient) tests, which assist in determining the likelihood of being on the autism spectrum. All the while I told myself that I was just going to see what it says—for fun.

Deep in the back of my mind I was confirming what I had already known, what I had already seen on paper—I am autistic. I tried to deny it but could not deny that I fit every single one of the diagnostic criteria for Asperger's Syndrome. I had previously been diagnosed with Sensory Processing Disorder (SPD) which is prevalent in those of us on the autism spectrum—in fact, in the new diagnostic criteria hypo or hyper-sensitivities is now a criterion in and of itself.

I could not deny that I displayed characteristically autistic behaviors as a child, and as an adult—although I was not able to put a name to the behaviors before this time. I could deny my feelings—but facts, those were plain to see.

I sat curled up on my recliner with my knees pulled into my chest. Tears flowed down my cheeks as I read about myself in book after book about Asperger's Syndrome. I saw myself, and I watched the tears fall. Why hadn't anyone seen it? Why didn't they tell me? Why was I in tears?

I was glad to know finally what was "wrong" with me, what was baffling was why I cried each time I read another symptom that fit. Each time I read an account of how another autistic woman experienced life that was different from the rest of the world, I cried. The experiences were similar to mine, but I had no idea they were different from the rest of the world's experiences.

I had no idea that I processed sensory information—sights, sounds, smells, touch, differently than everyone else. I automatically assumed that if I heard all those buzzing sounds, or smelled every single odor that lingered, then so did everyone else around me. It never occurred to me that I was experiencing the world differently, but it did explain why others looked at me like I had four heads when I explained it to them.

My tears were tears of sadness. I grieved the life I didn't have, the life that I wanted, the life that could have been so different if only I had known more about myself. My tears were tears of anger; anger toward my parents for not caring enough to see me for me, for not bothering to bring me to the "right" doctors, for not understanding me. Anger at all the doctors who misdiagnosed me, who drugged me up with medication into insensibility and blamed me for being out of my mind.

I was angry that these so-called professionals, and there were many, who touched my life did not see my autism—maybe they did not want to see. After all, there is no magic pill to cure autism so they would not have been able to use their prescription pad to make my symptoms magically disappear.

I cried tears of relief because I finally knew that I was not completely crazy. Relief that my sensory overloads were not "all in my head" as was suggested by my neurologist who should have known better. I was relieved to finally know that my difficulty interacting with the world around me, and my inability to connect with other people was not a personal flaw—a personal failure. In this regard, my realization of the truth was both a blessing and a curse.

It was a blessing to know that all my failed attempts at socialization, and making new friends in new places were not all my fault. A curse to finally realize that what I was trying and failing at over and over was not going to work the next time around. It was not going to change; I was not going to change. My loneliness may last forever, and that, my friend, is depressing.

Children and adults on the autism spectrum are prone to depression—I certainly am. Research has shown that nearly 65% of people with autism or Asperger's Syndrome present with symptoms of depression. The depression usually develops in late adolescence and early adulthood. This comes as no surprise to me. Those are the years that social interaction and life demands change rapidly and can often overwhelm us.

Due to the inability to express our emotions or communicate feelings of disturbance, anxiety or distress verbally, depression is often missed until it is so severe that it hinders our ability to function. I faxed my doctor a list of symptoms because I could not verbalize them when I was in his presence. I thought I had found a way to express my emotional state—through the written word, but he thought that made me a little crazy.

An autistic person with depression may not "appear" depressed to a physician that only see them once every couple of months due their impairment in non-verbal expression. My medical records are filled with this two word comment: Inappropriate affect.

Inappropriate affect is when a person is saying one thing with their words but their facial expressions, or body language is conveying a different story. When I finally found my words and was able to explain my feelings of depression and despair, I did so smiling. I was unaware that I was smiling; it certainly was not a smile of happiness—more likely it was anxiety slipping past my facade. When I am anxious I tend to smile, and make jokes (most of which no one else in the room seems to "get").

Many physicians commented that I conveyed happy events looking gloomy, and I conveyed very troubling events and feelings that "would bother most other people," but I was "cheerful, almost giddy." The particular physician who wrote this comment in my records determined that I was simply lying. That because my affect was inappropriate, it was a sign that I was being untruthful—nothing could have been further from the truth.

A minimum of four physicians, one general practitioner, two psychiatrists, and a neurologist, noted that I displayed inappropriate affect consistently, and none of them put the pieces of my puzzle together. The general practitioner sent me for a psych evaluation, the first psychiatrist decided I had major depression and panic anxiety disorder (by this time I most certainly did), the second psychiatrist determined I was a liar, and the neurologist—that I was crazy and my sensory processing issues were "all in my head."

It is no wonder that I had tears of relief to find out, finally, the truth—to discover an explanation, a diagnosis that explained not one or two of my symptoms or behaviors but ALL of them. Finally, someone saw *me*.

Despite my feelings of relief at receiving a proper diagnosis, depression began to set in. The thoughts of all the needless pain, all the missed opportunities, all the things if only I'd known I could have done differently were hard to banish.

The difference this time was that the depression did not stay very long. I rapidly found a way to communicate with other people like me—with other autistic adults.

I had never been a big fan of online communications, did not have a Facebook page or Twitter account, and had very little use for technology like smart phones—but now all that has changed. The communities and friendships that I have found online with other autistic adults helped me move quickly from depression to learning to accept my "condition."

The more I learned about autism, the more I needed to know. I researched, and read—a lot. Then I began to write. Writing—being able to communicate what I could never say with my spoken words has been a freeing and exhilarating experience.

Writing is my form of communication. I may not call someone on the telephone; I cannot stand to talk on the phone. I may not visit, make play dates, or organize night's out with friends, but I will, if they are willing—write. I will write messages, emails, and chat online—it is the easiest most honest way for me to communicate with the world.

Chapter Twenty-Three: Interacting With the World

Although I long for socialization like any other person, social situations often are overwhelming and hinder communication for many of us on the spectrum.

A simple invite to a coffee shop can be an overwhelming experience for an Aspie, those of us with Asperger's Syndrome. The coffee machine frothing, customers placing orders, the door opening and shutting letting in the distracting sounds from the outside are just a few of the background noises that my senses fail to filter out. All the sounds come at me at the same time, all wanting my immediate attention.

I desperately want to stick my orange and green foam earplugs into my ears, but that would be rude. Besides, they make me look the bride of Frankenstein. I slip my hand into my pocket and squish them between my fingers instead. The cushiony feel of them between my fingertips makes me feel better; a stress ball and security blanket in one.

Several women sit at the table sipping lattes and discussing their kids, the neighbor's new boyfriend, and the latest church gossip. It all sounds like noise, jumbled words that all blend together, and I cannot hone in on any one voice, on any one topic, or any one conversation. I fidget in my seat. I'm lost and I can't keep up, so I say nothing; I have no voice.

The sun shines through the glass sending blinding rays directly at our table; no one else notices. I slip my sunglasses over my eyes. We are just a tad too close to the restrooms, and when the door swings open the faint smell of urine mixes with the smell of cappuccino in the air. My stomach churns, jumps, and I try not to heave; no one else smells it.

The conversation fades into the background as I retreat into my own world. I have nothing to contribute, no idle chitchat to add. My mind is wondering—contemplating the next chapter of my book, my next blog post, the mound of books that I want to get back home to read. Back home to my computer screen. I love my computer—all my friends live in there, the people who I can talk to, the ones like me, the ones who understand me.

My cellphone dings, and I smile on the inside. I steal a glance at the phone; *do not be rude!* A little square green face pops onto the screen. I know I received a text message. Another ding, a small envelope—an email is waiting. A tiny pastel blue bird chirps—a new tweet mentioned me. The royal blue "F" indicating a new Facebook message or comment has my fingers tapping the screen, forgetting where I am. *What do my virtual friends have to say?*

Their words are in black and white, I can read them, process them, take a breath, and think about what I would like to say. I respond in my time, without pressure, without chitchat, with earplugs in, with quiet contemplation. They speak in turn, one message to read at a time, and if I miss a word I can go back and reread it again. No strange looks for wearing my sunglasses indoors, or odd stares because I didn't get the joke. If I am overwhelmed I don't have to respond immediately; I can breathe; I can be me.

In my virtual world I have a voice. I can "talk" without worrying about how I sound, if I spoke out of turn, or unwittingly offended someone. I can put my words to the page in a logical order, say what I mean, and mean what I say. In my fake world I am real, I am alive, and I have something worthwhile to say. In the real world, I am fake, voiceless, a mannequin, posing, pretending to fit in. I grasp for logic, meaning, and order—but there is none.

The conversation died down, but I hadn't noticed. Purses were gathered, and coffee cups cleared. "We'll have to do this again soon," followed by a polite smile. Was she talking to me? Soon? How soon, when?

"Um, Ok," I say. I sling the strap to my purple purse across my shoulder, unclip my car keys from the belt loop on my jeans, grab my phone from the table, stick it into my back pocket, and head for the door—glad that my coffee with strangers is over. Exhausted.

The next time I am invited to attend, I say I will, but don't show up.

"Everyone knows Jeannie; she just doesn't know them."

That was the common phrase I heard in high school. A constant stream of hugs, smiles, and waves filled my days. I never understood how so many people who I didn't know, knew me.

Prosopagnosia, also known as "facial agnosia" or "face-blindness," is a neurological disorder that makes facial recognition difficult or impossible. Two thirds of autistic children and adults have some degree of face-blindness. I live among those numbers.

Do I know you? That is the question that runs through my head when someone I don't recognize approaches me in public. They call me by name, ask about my children, my parents, and my work—I know I should know this person, but I do not.

When my husband and I were first married we attended a very large church in Brooklyn, New York where I often spoke to people having no idea who they were. I didn't think there was anything wrong with me. I just figured that in such a large church I never ran into the same person twice.

Being greeted by hugs and kisses from strangers has always made me uncomfortable; I don't like to be touched. To add to my discomfort the odd looks these strangers gave me when I introduced myself was unnerving. When people approached us to talk, I assumed that my husband knew them. We talked for a while, they left, and my husband would say, "You know them, I introduced you last week." You did?

I met the same people at church, each Sunday, talked with them, and still did not recognize them the following week. It's no wonder they looked at me like I was a lunatic when I introduced myself, yet again.

When the same scene played itself out over and over, I began to believe what I had been told my entire life. I was a lazy, absent-minded, self-absorbed air-head, who didn't care enough about people to remember them. Or—I was stuck up, obnoxious, too good for anyone, and just ignored people; nothing could have been further from the truth.

The first time I read about face-blindness, I was stunned. I had another one of those "ah ha" moments. The moments were I had to look back at my life with new eyes, evaluating it through the lens of autism.

It took 38 years for me to be diagnosed with Asperger's Syndrome (AS), a form of high functioning autism—38 years of confusing experiences.

When I was a child AS was not a known diagnosis in the United States. Although well-known in Europe for more than twenty years at the time, it only became a viable diagnosis in the U.S. in 1994; three years after I was out of high school, and two years after I'd dropped out of college the first time around.

What is wrong with me? Why do I have trouble recognizing faces?

We do not see with our eyes, we "see" with our brains. All of us—with or without autism see with our brains. Our eyes take in a snapshot but it is our brains that process all the information in the photo. It makes sense of all the patterns, categorizes them, and stores them for later use (recognition).

I fail to recognize familiar faces, but I never fail to recognize a tree, or a cat, or the shapes of clouds. Why?

A number of theories have arisen to answer this question. Maybe because we tend to not look people in the eye, or focus on their faces, we have a hard time remembering them. It is said that autistics tend to be socially uninterested—that we don't care enough to remember people.

Could it be an issue of weak central coherence?

Those with weak central coherence tend to focus on details but lose track of, or don't perceive the whole. A tendency to focus on minute details, a portion of the face or specific feature, without taking in the whole picture could be partially responsible for many autistics having difficulty with facial recognition. All of these theories seem viable; however, I believe there is more to it than that.

Facial recognition is isolated in the right temporal lobe in the "fusiform face area." Non-facial recognition happens on the left side of the brain. In other words, all other details, pieces, and patterns are processed on the left side of the brain.

Why does this matter? Autistics tend to do fairly well on pattern recognition tests—significantly better than their neuro-typical counterparts, but do poorly on facial recognition tests. The opposite is true for neuro-typical people who perform very well on facial recognition test, but do poorly in pattern recognition. In the autistic brain it seems that the "fusiform face area" does not function the way other people's do. This could explain why I wouldn't recognize you if you stood on your head—or would I?

Tests showed that autistics were able to recognize faces that they viewed upside down. Researchers found that the circuitry that recognizes faces only works on faces that are right side up. Upside down faces are routed to the left side of the brain to be processed like any other image. The upside down faces processed like patterns, and autistics recognized those facial patterns.

"How did you know it was me?" a friend asked pulling her mask from her face.

Costume parties, for me, are like any other social gathering. If I knew you well, I recognized you. It did not matter what you used to cover your face. I recognized the contour of my friend's hands, her ring, the shoes we bought at the mall that summer, the way she stood, and swished her head back and forth when she talked. I spotted her from across the room, without hearing her say a word, or knowing what costume she was wearing.

Most people rely on facial features to recognize someone they know. I've always wondered why bank robbers wore ski masks, but did not disguise the rest of the body. And it was ridiculous that in superhero movies no one recognized their loved ones because they wore a mask over their face. Don't all people rely on other details to recognize people they know?

When I think of my brother, I can form a mental picture of his face in my mind. I have no problem recognizing people who I know well. But I can also bring up just as sharp mental picture of his hands, or the way he has this one thick vein that rolls back and forth over his wrist bone. My oldest brother has hands exactly like my mother's, my father's hands look exactly like his fathers, and my son's feet are very similar to my youngest brother's feet. I would recognize the way the hair lies across my husband's arms, and would recognize him even if he wore a mask. These details are as vivid as any face I can recall.

For several years I worked in prisons. My co-workers often wore uniforms, and were stationed at the same posts day after day. On a daily basis, I recognized them, said hello, knew their names— but if I saw them outside work, I did not recognize them. If their uniform was off, or they were not where they should be (at their post), then I did not recognize them. I processed the whole situation—the person, in uniform, sitting behind that desk. I was not processing the person's face. Place this same person in the supermarket, at the post office, or in the school cafeteria eating with their children, and I do not recognize them at all.

Many people have had the experience of seeing someone, and not being able to "place" their face; they the person who stands before them from somewhere, but can't remember where. Or, they know the face and cannot recall a name. I too, have had these types of experiences with those that I have had contact with often enough to recognize something about them. But—more often than not, I simple do not recognize them at all. There is no inkling of familiarity, no spark of recognition; it is as if I am staring into the face of a complete and total stranger.

When I see people out of context, somewhere I do not expect them to be, someone I have not seen often, or someone I have not seen in a long time I will not recognize them. I will stroll past them in the supermarket just as I would anyone else I didn't know. Many times this will cause people to think that I am ignoring them—on purpose, when the truth is I didn't even know I knew them.

I continually have difficulty recognizing my son's teachers at school despite the fact that I see them where I *expect* to, and that I've meet them several times. This year, after discovering my degree of face-blindness, I set out to remember what my son's teacher looked like.

The first time I met her, she must have thought there was something seriously wrong with me. She spoke, and I stared. I caught myself noticing the color of her hair, and the style in which she had it brushed, her outfit, even her shoes but I rarely looked at her face. I adjusted.

I purposed to look directly at her face while she was speaking to me. Up until this point I was not consciously aware of how uncomfortable looking someone in the eye really was, but I was determined, so I persisted. I studied her. I registered her blue eyes, and her narrow nose—all individual features. Surely if I could memorize these features I would recognize her the next time I came to school.

Unfortunately my stare-feast was unsuccessful. Not only did I not recognize the woman the next time I visited my son's classroom, but I also did not hear a word she said while talking to me. I was studying her, concentrating on her features, but her words never registered in my mind. I have absolutely no idea what she talked to me about. I left utterly confused, exhausted, and uncomfortable from the effort, and it didn't even help me recognize her face the next time around—frustrating.

I do not know how much contact I need to have with a person in order for their faces to be permanently branded into my memory, but I know it must be a lot. I must know a person very well in order to recognize them even after a long absence. Apparently, just frequent contact is not enough to sustain a working facial memory.

When I lived in a small town in South Carolina, I attended the same church for nearly two years. I recognized the people I had contact with at church frequently. I even began to recognize them in other places around town. However, several years later, living in a different South Carolina city, I ran into these same people from time to time, mostly at the mall, and had no spark of recognition.

My husband and I usually stop and he chit chats for a while. I answer some questions, and when we walk away he promptly informs me of where I know the person from. I think that I have become adept at chatting without letting on that I have no idea who I am talking to or why they are talking to me, but I could be wrong. My husband says that I get that "blank look" on my face, and he knows immediately that I don't recognize to whom I am speaking.

The knowledge of my autism has changed my perception, and allowed me to look with a new pair of eyes, with new lenses that filter everything through the knowledge of autism. That has been an eye-opening experience. Not a day goes by where I don't learn something new about myself, about my life, my mind, my senses, and of course, my ASD children.

Growing up without knowing what was "wrong" with me was painful, but nothing compared to navigating adulthood. Many of my autistic traits that were readily apparent in childhood became masked in adolescence, but exacerbated in adulthood. When I was younger I "looked" autistic, as an older adult I again am beginning to "look" autistic.

The stresses and pressures of an adult life, family, marriage, children, and financial burdens put pressure on my ability to cope. I suppose I may be just too tired to pretend to be normal; too tired to consciously stop each instance of stimming, or every impending meltdown. I become more easily overloaded by sights, sounds, and smells than I was even a few years ago. My sensory processing issues seem more severe.

As a child, I was carefree—happy, as I knew happy to be at the time. But when I grew into a young woman life got messy, and continued to come unraveled as time went on. I had difficulty making friends, raising children, and communicating with my husband largely due to my autism.

Not that my autism itself was to blame exactly, but my

misunderstanding of myself, and my continual misjudgment of others. I still have difficulty understanding others, and judging their actions and motives, but now I have a microscope to look at a situation with—a microscope that I know how to properly configure in order to evaluate my life.

The beauty of finally receiving a proper diagnosis is that I have been able to connect to the world, to people like me, to other "Aspies". I have been able to share my experiences without eyebrows raised and people looking at me like I am from Mars. I now treasure these people who not only listen to my rambling, but help me to understand more about myself and to know for the first time in my life that I truly am not alone.

The knowledge of my autism has helped me in so many ways. For a person with autism or Asperger's Syndrome, not knowing anything is a form of torture in and of itself. So finally having a name, a definition, that I can apply to myself has helped tremendously and been of incalculable worth to me.

My boys now know I'm an Aspie, and to my 2 year old I'm still just Mama. To my 8 year-old Aspie son, I'm still just mom. To my 13 year old Aspie son, I am part mom, part superhero (according to him, my super-senses are super-powers). I am still the same person my husband fell in love with and married, but now we are learning more about autism together. We are learning how to communicate and understand each other better

Our life is not perfect, but the veil of darkness and misunderstanding has been pulled from our eyes. I will never be "normal" as in Neuro-typical, but I am normal for me. Now more than ever before I am starting to learn just who I am, which would not have happened without my official autism diagnosis.

My differences define me. My quirks are now explainable.

Knowing why something affects me the way it does, allows me to find ways to cope and sometimes even counter some of the more negative traits that come along with my autism.

I have Asperger's Syndrome. I am an Aspergirl, I am a mom, I am a wife, and I am an individual who sees things in a unique way. I am just like you, only different because I am me. Now I know being me is not a bad thing.

I rejoice in my Aspie-ness, and if you are on the spectrum, or someone you love is, you should too.

Author's Notes; My Beloved Aspie Label

Before I had completed writing Twirling Naked in the Streets, the DSM underwent yet another change; Asperger's Syndrome (AS), will be removed from the *Diagnostic and Statistical Manual of Mental Disorders* (DSM-5), which will be published and in effect in May of 2013.AS will now be included under the umbrella diagnosis of Autism Spectrum Disorder (ASD). ASD will encompass Asperger's Syndrome, Autistic Disorder, and PPD-NOS—all autism spectrum disorders.

To be honest I am torn about the new DSM-V. On one hand I have finally found out what has been "wrong" with me my entire life. Being diagnosed with Asperger's Syndrome came as quite a shock to me and many others, but in reality when the shock wore off, it was a tremendous relief.

I finally had a name for my difficulties. This will not change under the new DSM-V because I am clearly within the new diagnostic guidelines for Autism Spectrum Disorder. In fact, I actually fit those criteria more accurately than the previous.

The part that concerns me most is the removing of the name, Asperger's Syndrome. I understand that we as people are not a name, but it almost feels like invalidation. For 38 years I did not exist, no one saw my autism/Asperger's, and now on some level I feel like it has happened again. I finally had a group of people to which I belonged, to identify with (Aspies), and the label has been removed.

Under the new diagnostic criteria outlined in the DSM-V, in order for a person to be diagnosed with Autism Spectrum Disorder (ASD), individuals "must meet criteria A, B, C, and D.

A. Persistent deficits in social communication and social interaction across contexts, not accounted for by general developmental delays, and manifest <u>by all 3 of the following</u>:

1. <u>Deficits in social-emotional reciprocity</u>; *ranging from abnormal social approach* and failure of normal back and forth conversation through reduced sharing of interests, emotions, and affect and response to total lack of initiation of social interaction,

2. <u>Deficits in nonverbal communicative behaviors used for social interaction</u>; ranging from poorly integrated-verbal and nonverbal communication, through abnormalities in eye contact and body-language, or deficits in understanding the use of nonverbal communication, to total lack of facial expression or gestures.

3. <u>Deficits in developing and maintaining relationships</u>, appropriate to developmental level (beyond those with caregivers); ranging from difficulties adjusting behavior to suit different social contexts through difficulties in sharing imaginative play and in making friends to an apparent absence of interest in people

B. Restricted, repetitive patterns of behavior, interests, or activities as manifested by at <u>least two of the following</u>:

1. Stereotyped or repetitive speech, motor movements, or use of objects (such as simple motor stereotypies, echolalia, repetitive use of objects, or idiosyncratic phrases);

2. Excessive adherence to routines, ritualized patterns of verbal or nonverbal behavior, or excessive resistance to change; (such as motoric rituals, insistence on same route or food, repetitive questioning or extreme distress at small changes);

3. Highly restricted, fixated interests that are abnormal in intensity or focus (such as strong attachment to or preoccupation with unusual objects, excessively circumscribed or perseverative interests);

4. ** Hyper-or hypo-reactivity to sensory input or unusual interest in sensory aspects of environment (such as apparent indifference to pain/heat/cold, adverse response to specific sounds or textures, excessive smelling or touching of objects, fascination with lights or spinning objects); (*emphasis mine*)

**This is new

C. <u>Symptoms must be present in early childhood (but may not become fully manifest until social demands exceed limited capacities)</u>

D. <u>Symptoms together limit and impair everyday functioning</u>."

I have highlighted above some the most important things about this criterion, and what I consider to be the most concerning. To begin with, the first section, A, highlights social interactions and to receive/maintain a diagnosis of autism spectrum disorder, you must meet ALL THREE OF THE DEFICITS highlighted. It bothers me that autism is still being categorized so strongly as a mainly communication disorder because socializing is only the tip of the iceberg when we look at autism as a whole.

There has been some concern from adults and parents of children with Asperger's Syndrome that they may lose their diagnosis, thereby losing their support with school systems, and medical communities. I believe that you have a diagnosis anywhere on the spectrum you will likely retain that diagnosis even given the three socialization based criteria, which uses broad non-specific language. The language gives doctors much latitude in diagnosis. Who is to say what *abnormal social approach* is? What exactly is normal?

I think that we have an improvement of sorts in section B, where patients are required to exhibit two of the four symptoms listed. This is the first time that *hyper-or-hypo reactivity to sensory input* has been included in autism diagnostic criteria.

I am happy to see this added with the hope that the medical profession may be beginning to see this part of our difficulties. If I had to pick just one aspect of my autism that gives me the most trouble, is the most disabling, it would be my sensory issues—no contest.
I suspect the same is true for many spectrum children. From my experience, I can tell you that many meltdowns, "temper tantrums", outbursts and complete shutdowns, where I've closed myself off from the world, were directly connected to the amount of sensory overload I experienced.

The final two sections lists in the criterion simply state that symptoms must have been present from early childhood, and interfere with everyday function. If you have read all the way through this book to this point, you can plainly see that both criteria have easily met.

I, along with many other Aspies, will not be "losing" our autism diagnoses; we will only be losing a label. Albeit, this is a label that was hard to come by, difficult to understand, and has taken a long time to accept. Now that it is a part of me, and has helped me understand myself, and connect with others more easily, I will be sad to see it go.

About the Author

Jeannie Davide-Rivera is a student, writer, wife, and mother with Asperger's Syndrome. She lives in South Carolina with her husband, and their three sons, who are all on the autism spectrum.

You can visit her Asperger's Website at:

www.aspiewriter.com

Connect with the author through her personal Facebook page

www.facebook.com/aspiewriter

Follow her on Twitter:

https://twitter.com/AspieWriter

45382750R00115

Made in the USA
Middletown, DE
02 July 2017